DATE DUE		

COMPREHENSIVE RESEARCH
AND STUDY GUIDE

BLOOM'S
MAJOR
SHORT STORY
WRITERS

Sherwood

Anderson

**EDITED AND WITH AN
INTRODUCTION BY HAROLD BLOOM**

CURRENTLY AVAILABLE

BLOOM'S MAJOR DRAMATISTS

Aeschylus
Aristophanes
Bertolt Brecht
Anton Chekhov
Euripides
Henrik Ibsen
Eugène Ionesco
Ben Johnson
Christopher
  Marlowe
Arthur Miller
Eugene O'Neill
Luigi Pirandello
Shakespeare's
  Comedies
Shakespeare's
  Histories
Shakespeare's
  Romances
Shakespeare's
  Tragedies
George Bernard
  Shaw
Sam Shepard
Neil Simon
Oscar Wilde
Thornton Wilder
Tennessee
  Williams
August Wilson

BLOOM'S MAJOR NOVELISTS

Jane Austen
The Brontës
Willa Cather
Stephen Crane
Charles Dickens
Fyodor Dostoevsky
William Faulkner
F. Scott Fitzgerald
Thomas Hardy
Nathaniel Hawthorne
Ernest Hemingway
Henry James
James Joyce
Franz Kafka
D. H. Lawrence
Herman Melville
Toni Morrison
Marcel Proust
John Steinbeck
Stendhal
Leo Tolstoy
Mark Twain
Alice Walker
Edith Wharton
Virginia Woolf

BLOOM'S MAJOR POETS

Maya Angelou
Elizabeth Bishop
William Blake
Gwendolyn Brooks
Robert Browning
Geoffrey Chaucer
Sameul Taylor
  Coleridge
Dante
Emily Dickinson
John Donne
H.D.
T. S. Eliot
Robert Frost
Seamus Heaney
Homer
Langston Hughes
John Keats
John Milton
Sylvia Plath
Edgar Allan Poe
Poets of World War I
Shakespeare's Poems
  & Sonnets
Percy Shelley
Alfred, Lord
  Tennyson
Walt Whitman
William Carlos Williams
William Wordsworth
William Butler Yeats

BLOOM'S MAJOR SHORT STORY WRITERS

Jorge Luis Borges
Italo Calvino
Raymond Carver
Anton Chekhov
Joseph Conrad
Stephen Crane
William Faulkner
F. Scott Fitzgerald
Nathaniel Hawthorne
Ernest Hemingway
O. Henry
Shirley Jackson
Henry James
James Joyce
Franz Kafka
D.H. Lawrence
Jack London
Thomas Mann
Herman Melville
Flannery O'Connor
Edgar Allan Poe
Katherine Anne Porter
J. D. Salinger
John Steinbeck
Mark Twain
John Updike
Eudora Welty

COMPREHENSIVE RESEARCH
AND STUDY GUIDE

BLOOM'S
MAJOR
SHORT STORY
WRITERS

Sherwood
Anderson

CHELSEA HOUSE
PUBLISHERS

A Haights Cross Communications Company

Philadelphia

EDITED AND WITH AN INTRODUCTION BY HAROLD BLOOM

A Haights Cross Communications ◀ Company

Printed and bound in the United States of America.

First Printing
1 3 5 7 9 8 6 4 2

Library of Congress Cataloging-in-Publication Data

Sherwood Anderson / edited with an introduction by Harold Bloom.
      p. cm. — (Bloom's major short story writers)
Includes bibliographical references (p.   ) and index.
    ISBN 0-7910-6820-X
   1. Anderson, Sherwood, 1876–1941—Criticism and interpretation. 2.
Short story. I. Bloom, Harold. II. Series.
   PS3501.N4 Z826 2002
   813'.52—dc21   2002009670

Chelsea House Publishers
1974 Sproul Road, Suite 400
Broomall, PA 19008-0914

http://www.chelseahouse.com

Contributing Editor: Janyce Marson

Cover design by Keith Trego

Layout by EJB Publishing Services

CONTENTS

USER'S GUIDE

This volume is designed to present biographical, critical, and bibliographical information on the author and the author's best-known or most important short stories. Following Harold Bloom's editor's note and introduction is a concise biography of the author that discusses major life events and important literary accomplishments. A critical analysis of each story follows, tracing significant themes, patterns, and motifs in the work. An annotated list of characters supplies brief information on the main characters in each story.

A selection of critical extracts, derived from previously published material, follows each thematic analysis. In most cases, these extracts represent the best analysis available from a number of leading critics. Because these extracts are derived from previously published material, they will include the original notations and references when available. Each extract is cited, and readers are encouraged to use the original publications as they continue their research. A bibliography of the author's writings, a list of additional books and articles on the author and their work, and an index of themes and ideas conclude the volume.

As with any study guide, this volume is designed as a supplement to the works being discussed, and is in no way intended as a replacement for those works. The reader is advised to read the text prior to using this study guide, and to keep it accessible for quick reference.

ABOUT THE EDITOR

Harold Bloom is Sterling Professor of the Humanities at Yale University and Henry W. and Albert A. Berg Professor of English at the New York University Graduate School. He is the author of over 20 books, and the editor of more than 30 anthologies of literary criticism.

Professor Bloom's works include *Shelley's Mythmaking* (1959), *The Visionary Company* (1961), *Blake's Apocalypse* (1963), *Yeats* (1970), *A Map of Misreading* (1975), *Kabbalah and Criticism* (1975), *Agon: Toward a Theory of Revisionism* (1982), *The American Religion* (1992), *The Western Canon* (1994), and *Omens of Millennium: The Gnosis of Angels, Dreams, and Resurrection* (1996). *The Anxiety of Influence* (1973) sets forth Professor Bloom's provocative theory of the literary relationships between the great writers and their predecessors. His most recent books include *Shakespeare: The Invention of the Human*, a 1998 National Book Award finalist, *How to Read and Why* (2000), and *Stories and Poems for Extremely Intelligent Children of All Ages* (2001).

Professor Bloom earned his Ph.D. from Yale University in 1955 and has served on the Yale faculty since then. He is a 1985 MacArthur Foundation Award recipient and served as the Charles Eliot Norton Professor of Poetry at Harvard University in 1987–88. In 1999 he was awarded the prestigious American Academy of Arts and Letters Gold Medal for Criticism. Professor Bloom is the editor of several other Chelsea House series in literary criticism, including BLOOM'S MAJOR SHORT STORY WRITERS, BLOOM'S MAJOR NOVELISTS, BLOOM'S MAJOR DRAMATISTS, BLOOM'S MODERN CRITICAL INTERPRETATIONS, BLOOM'S MODERN CRITICAL VIEWS, and BLOOM'S BIOCRITIQUES.

EDITOR'S NOTE

My Introduction muses on "Death in the Woods," Sherwood Anderson's most notorious story, and both praises it as achieved art and expresses a reservation about its vision of life.

I find useful all the Critical Views excerpted in this volume, but particularly commend Mary Anne Ferguson on the narrator of "Death in the Woods," as well as Irving Howe and Horace Gregory on the terror of the grotesque in "The Man Who Became a Woman."

"I Want to Know Why" is placed in its biographical context by Walter B. Rideout, while "The Egg" is elucidated with skill by Michael D. West.

INTRODUCTION
Harold Bloom

Historically, Sherwood Anderson was a considerable figure in the development of the American short story during the two decades of the Nineteen Twenties and Thirties. Influenced by the naturalism of Theodore Dreiser and the prose experimentalism of Gertrude Stein, Anderson developed a narrative art sufficiently his own so that he became a crucial, early influence upon Ernest Hemingway and William Faulkner, both of whom rather ungratefully satirized him.

Anderson's obsessive "grotesques," each trapped in his or her own perspective, are generally the protagonists of his most successful stories. But my own favorite among Anderson's tales, "Death in the Woods," concerns a lifelong victim, too minimal in consciousness to be considered a grotesque. A late story, published in 1933, "Death in the Woods," tells the melancholy saga of Ma Marvin, a poor, isolated old woman who has been exploited her whole life long. Anderson neither celebrates nor laments her, but transforms her into his incantatory prose poem: "a thing so complete has its own beauty." The narrator, plainly a surrogate for Anderson, experiences both his own incarnation as an artist and his simultaneous initial sexual arousal by beholding the frozen body of the old woman, strangely white and lovely, as though she were a young girl again.

Rereading "Death in the Woods," after first confronting (and teaching) it half a century ago, I find myself both impressed and chilled by it. By centering upon the narrator's vision of Ma Marvin's death, Anderson reduces her life to its aesthetic consequences, serving as material for the story. The narrator feeds upon the old woman much as humans and animals always have fed themselves upon her. One looks for some ironic awareness of the artist's culpability in "Death in the Woods," but the irony is not there. Its absence marks both Anderson's purity as a storyteller and his limitations as well.

BIOGRAPHY OF
Sherwood Anderson

Sherwood Anderson, born of Scotch-Irish ancestry in Camden, Ohio on September 13, 1876, was the third of three children to Irwin M. Anderson and Emma Smith. Anderson's father, a journeyman harness-maker, had a fondness for horses which was to figure very prominently in Sherwood Anderson's literary work. Mr. Anderson's business eventually failed, he began to drink heavily and, thus, Sherwood Anderson's childhood was an impoverished one—the children and their mother having to contribute to the family's well-being. In fact, Sherwood Anderson earned the nickname, "Jobby," because of his eagerness to do a variety of odd jobs. At various times, Anderson worked as a farmhand, a grocery delivery boy, a worker in a newly-established bicycle factory, a newsboy and a laborer in a racetrack stable. "For a time he was the chief newsboy in Clyde, swinging onto trains and soliciting passengers with a shouted headline and a friendly grin." Nevertheless, despite his father's irresponsible ways and the burden he caused the rest of his family, Sherwood's father did have some lovable attributes: He was a man who managed to maintain a cheerful disposition, a man who loved to tell stories to adults and children alike, and a man who, despite his financial hardship, never lost his interest in music, theatre and literature. Later in life, Anderson would become obsessed with his father's character, so much so that his father would play an important role in his thoughts and in his writing, especially in the character Windy McPherson.

Although Anderson was to a large extent self-educated, he was a serious thinker who had read widely and was one of the earliest writers to respond to the new psychological theories of Sigmund Freud, giving great credence to the concept of the reality of the unconscious mind as the possessor of secrets of the individual's otherwise "forgotten" past history. Indeed, one source of insurmountable frustration for Anderson's characters is their unsuccessful struggle to gain access to a hidden reality within themselves while, at the same time, struggling to find individual purpose when confronted with the reality of the machine age as well as the circumscribed existence of life in a conventional setting, both urban and small-town alike. Anderson received the usual public school education, and though he was an average student, his many jobs and responsibilities caused him to quit high school before graduating. At the age of sixteen or seventeen, Anderson left the family farm in Clyde, Ohio for Chicago, where he worked for four or five years as a manual laborer in a cold storage warehouse. However, during the Spanish-American War, Anderson volunteered for army duty in Cuba, arriving there in January 1899, approximately four months after hostilities ceased. The experience, however, made a lasting impression as he became very aware of the individual's plight in having to conform to a mass society.

Upon his return from the Spanish-American War, Anderson followed his brother, Karl, to Springfield, Ohio in 1900. At this juncture, Anderson determined that he needed to continue the education he never completed and enrolled, at the age of twenty-four, in the Wittenberg Academy, a preparatory school, where he proved himself a very able and diligent student, in such subjects as Latin, Greek, geometry, English and physics. Moreover, Anderson worked his way through school as a "chore" boy in the boardinghouse where he lived with Karl and various other editors, artists, advertising men and teachers.

The cultural and business environment of the boardinghouse residents opened up new worlds for Anderson. Through the intercession of the advertising manager for Crowell Publishing Company, where Karl worked as an artist, Anderson was appointed to the Chicago advertising office of the firm as a copywriter. Anderson did well in this job and when he became an advertising salesman, others were drawn to him by his physical attractiveness, lively spirit, and charming personality. In a series of articles and sketches he wrote in 1903 and 1904 for *Agricultural Advertising*, the firm's house publication, Anderson espoused the basic tenets of popular American business philosophy, such as the virtue of hard work, competition, acquisition, optimism, and success.

In 1904, Anderson married Cornelia Lane, the daughter of a wealthy Ohio businessman. The couple spent their honeymoon in Tennessee, where they visited the St. Louis World's Fair. While Cornelia had earned a degree from Western Reserve University, with a background in literature and the arts, Anderson lacked this requisite training and his resulting frustration caused him to turn his aspirations to literary endeavors. Furthermore, Anderson had always possessed a reverent attitude toward language and, later on, he would become obsessed by words. Indeed, one of the many literary influences on his writing was the writings of Gertrude Stein's and her experiments with language in *Tender Buttons*. His admiration for *Tender Buttons* is expressed in *A Story Teller's Story*: "How it excited me! Here was something purely experimental and dealing in words separated from sense ... an approach I am sure the poets must often be compelled to make." From Anderson's perspective, Stein was a pioneer in her abandonment of conventional syntax, punctuation and spelling, a writer who eschewed the dead language of conformity to literary custom.

In 1906, Anderson moved to Cleveland and became the head of a mail-order business and in 1907 he moved to Elyria, Ohio where he became the head of a mail-order paint company. It was also in 1907 that his first son, Robert Lane, was born. Anderson would remain in Elyria for the next five years; a second son, John Sherwood, would be born in 1908, and a daughter, Marion, in 1911. In Elyria, Anderson strove to balance a bourgeois lifestyle of church attendance and country club membership, while secretly pursuing his literary work at home during the night and later, openly, in the office and elsewhere. One result of the feverish pitch at which he worked was an increasing estrangement from his wife in addition to financial difficulties. On November 27, 1912, Anderson precipitately left his office in Elyria, Ohio and was not heard from again until he was taken to a Cleveland hospital where his condition was diagnosed as mental collapse. This crisis was a turning point in his life and, after leaving the hospital, he took his family in 1913 to Chicago where he returned to his previous advertising job and continued to excel as a copywriter until 1922. However, on his return to Chicago, he also brought with him the manuscripts of *Windy McPherson's Son* (a novel in which the protagonist searches for, but does not discover, the meaning of life) and *Marching Men* (a social novel concerned with the dehumanizing effects of industrialism in Pennsylvania) in addition to other work. Anderson's perspective on his departure from Elyria is set forth in an article entitled "When I Left Business for Literature," which appeared in the *Century* in 1924. Although Anderson would ultimately ignore his breakdown and financial setback, he was truthful about the artistic motivation that led him to forsake a conventional life and immerse himself in an artistic one. Life in the big city of Chicago would help him to divest any illusions about a career in advertising, while at the same time, help him in fostering his aesthetic ideas and literary aspirations.

During his time in Chicago, Anderson had several other literary successes. In the late fall of 1915, Sherwood Anderson began writing the stories that comprise *Winesburg, Ohio*. These stories, though written expeditiously, went through a series of careful and sustained revisions with the result that in 1919 *Winesburg, Ohio* won international acclaim for its insightful and penetrating psychological study of and compassion for the suffering and warped personalities of the characters. In 1916, Anderson divorced Cornelia Lane and married Tennessee Mitchell with the understanding that the two would be able to come and go as their careers required. Anderson had met Tennessee in the summer of 1916 where she had been attending a camp for modern dancing directed by Alys Bentley in the Adirondacks. Nevertheless, their marriage was a rocky one and would eventually end in divorce in 1924.

In 1921, Anderson was awarded *The Dial* prize of two thousand dollars, the purpose of which was to further the work of the American author most deserving of encouragement and support. That same year he met Gertrude Stein in Europe and William Faulkner in New Orleans. Gertrude Stein's influence was far-reaching and the regular guests at her famous salon, whom Anderson met, included many of the most important literary men of the time, among them Ezra Pound, T.S. Eliot, James Joyce and Ernest Hemingway.

In 1924, Anderson married his third wife, Elizabeth Prall, a small, quiet, and introverted woman, originally from Saginaw, Michigan, Prall graduated from the University of Michigan at Ann Arbor and then continued on to New York to attend the

Public Library School for librarians, and where she managed the Lord & Taylor bookstore. It was through this position that she met Sherwood Anderson and was impressed by his confident personality. Sherwood was, in turn, attracted to her education and stable family background. During the fall months in New York, Anderson took Elizabeth to concerts, theatres and parties. Anderson and Prall would eventually divorce in 1932. It was also during this time that Anderson met Alfred Stieglitz, the famous photographer and art patron, with whom he became a close friend. Above all, Anderson admired Stieglitz's artistic integrity, a true craftsman.

During the 1920's Anderson was preoccupied with his own literary endeavors and had little interest in politics, though his natural sympathies were for the working class. In 1927, he moved to Troutdale, Virginia and purchased two newspapers in Marion. The events of 1929, however, with the stock market crash, the resulting depression and the terrible national tragedy of a wave of suicides, caused Anderson to become interested in proletarian movements and to examine his own lifestyle. While traveling in the South in the early 1930's, Anderson drove through small Georgia mill towns and observed the problems of the machine age and the ways in which industrialism damaged man's spirit and severed him from the sense of a sense of pride and accomplishment. Furthermore, he was also struck by the plight of the mill women who reminded him of his hardworking mother. With this memory of his mother firmly in his mind, Anderson fell in love once again, this time with Eleanor Copenhaver, a well-educated woman who had done two years of graduate work at Bryn Mawr and who pursued her industrial interests by becoming the Industrial Secretary of the YWCA. As a result of her position, Eleanor was able to further educate Anderson as to the problems of women factory workers. Anderson would eventually marry Eleanor Copenhaver in 1933. And, as a result of this love affair, Anderson attempted to divest himself of all property.

However, it was the Danville, Virginia mill strike that would have the most profound influence on Anderson's thinking, where he made a speech to the workers in January 1931 encouraging them to continue their struggle. "You are fighting as men and women for the right to stand up, to lead decent lives, to breathe deeper, to save your manhood and your womanhood." During the 1930's Anderson, like many other liberals witnessing the demoralizing effects of unemployment and society's responsibility for causing these problems in its pursuit of money and reliance on modern machinery, looked to communism as a cure. Nevertheless, he was concerned by the dogmatism of some of its advocates and always saw himself as an artist apart from the rank and file communists.

Anderson's life ended in 1941, his final decade bringing him happiness in his marriage to Eleanor, whose selfless devotion to Sherwood's happiness and wanderlust made their relationship a successful one. On February 28, 1941, Anderson embarked upon a goodwill tour of South America, in part a respite from the tensions of World War II. But Anderson became sick with peritonitis while on board ship, the result of swallowing a small piece of toothpick during a farewell cocktail party. Anderson died on March 8 at Colon, Panama and was buried in Marion, Virginia on March 26.

A NOTE ON THE

Grotesque

The "Book of the Grotesque," the concept of which was to influence all of Anderson's writing and has since received an enormous amount of critical response, is the inaugural story of *Winesburg, Ohio*. It was first published in 1915, along with the story "Hands," in the periodical *Masses*. Perhaps it is more accurate to refer to the "Book of the Grotesque" as Anderson's prefatory statement concerning his theory of human character. Here, the narrator tells us that he had once had the opportunity of seeing a book written by an old man on the subject of the grotesque in human nature. It is important to note that the word grotesque is derived from the word grotto because on the walls of caves ancient artists would often draw representations of distorted, exaggerated, and even ugly, human figures. However, Anderson was not interested in physical appearance but, rather, a grotesqueness from within—borne of an individual seizing on a single aspect of a larger truth and allowing that overly-simplified perspective to become the overwhelming reality that dictates his behavior and thought patterns. As the narrator tells us, "[t]he old man had listed hundreds of truths in his book.... There was the truth of virginity and the truth of passion, the truth of wealth and of poverty, of thrift and of profligacy, of carefulness and abandon." While all of these truths are valuable and important, human beings go wrong in attaching themselves to one particular truth to the exclusion of all others. Thus, in one sense, a "grotesque" is one who has a very limited and circumscribed perspective, in which said narrow perspective will work to his detriment. "It was [the old man's] notion that the moment one of the people took one of the truths to himself, called it his truth, and tried to live his life by it, he became a grotesque and the truth he embraced a falsehood."

In his biography of Sherwood Anderson, James Schevill discusses the "grotesque" as part of Anderson's myth-making in *Winesburg, Ohio*, the town represented in the popular tradition as the lazy, gentle village of the Christian virtues." As Schevill goes on to explain, the "grotesques" are "universal people, defeated by their false ideas and dreams.... The 'grotesque' is neither misshapen nor abnormal. He is an unintegrated personality, cut off from society and adrift in his own mind." In other words, Anderson has given a new dimension of meaning to conventional definitions of the grotesque, his own unique paradigm for explaining the trap that so many of his characters have unwittingly and inescapably fallen into. Anderson's characters live out the tragedy of modern life, a death in life, devoid of any real identity or hope of redemption.

CRITICAL VIEWS ON
Winesburg, Ohio

DAVID D. ANDERSON ON THE DESIRE FOR PERMANENCE

[David D. Anderson is the author of "Sherwood Anderson's Midwest and the Industrial South in *Beyond Desire*" (1999) and "The Chicago Renaissance in Fiction" (1999). In the following excerpt from his article, "Wanderers and Sojourners: Sherwood Anderson and the People of Winesburg," Anderson discusses the characters' desire for permanence.]

Winesburg, Ohio is indeed a testament, as all of Anderson's work is a testament to his time and place, and, like Thoreau's Walden, Faulkner's Yoknapatawpha County, and Hemingway's Northern Michigan, the mythical town of Winesburg is one of the most enduring places in American literature. So vivid is the place of Winesburg in the pages of the book and so sharply etched is it in the American literary imagination and the collective American memory of a long-lost past that we overlook the fact that Winesburg, Ohio, like all American literary places, is a manifestation of a literal past and present marked not by stability and permanence but by movement, chance, and transience. Winesburg, Ohio, like the Clyde, Ohio, and the Old Northwest recently become the Midwest of Anderson's youth, was not a goal or an end in itself for its people; rather it was a way station, a place to which one came to find refuge or to await an opportunity to move on, or conversely, a place in which one was forced by circumstances to live and die alone. Winesburg, like Anderson's Clyde, like the America that was by Anderson's time more than five hundred years old in the Anglo-American memory and imagination, is a place uniquely suited not for those who seek stability and permanence but for those who, as sojourners and wanderers, arrive, stay, and move on, if not in the course of their lives, certainly in their hopes, dreams, and imaginations.

In their roles as sojourners and wanderers, the people of Winesburg have much in common with their creator. Sherwood Anderson is, like the town of his memory and creative imagination as well as the story-telling talent that defined the twisted lives of Winesburg's people, firmly associated with the American small town, so much so that in *Home Town*, his last work published in his lifetime, he admitted that he "must be an incurable small-town man." But much of his active life had taken place in cities—in Chicago, to which he went to live three times, in Cleveland and Elyria, Ohio, where he pursued business success, and in New York and New Orleans—before he found Marion and Troutdale, Virginia, as the base from which he carried on the almost ceaseless wandering that marked his last years, culminating in his death in Colon, Panama Canal Zone, on March 8, 1941.

From his departure from Clyde, Ohio, at twenty in 1896 to his death in Panama forty-five years later, Anderson's life consisted of two major phases, that until early 1913, during which he shared the values of his age and pursued business success, and the last twenty-eight years of his life, which were spent as a wanderer, an observer, a sojourner, and a teller of tales, a life increasingly dominated not by his association with the small town but by his perception of himself as a conscious literary artist. (...)

The Clyde, Ohio, that had become part of Anderson's memory and the substance of his literary imagination was not only the basis of *Winesburg, Ohio*, but of his first major publication, *Windy McPherson's Son* in 1916 as well as of *Home Town*, the last in his lifetime, in 1940, and a good number of works between them. It was also the Clyde of the twenty years from 1884 to 1886, of the 2380 people who lived there in 1880, of the few more in 1890 and in 1900. Those numbers represented the people, together with those in his Chicago boarding house and later in the Army and in the town of Elyria, who peopled his memory and his literary imagination and who were to become the wanderers and sojourners of Winesburg, Ohio, the place, the refuge, the way station, and the point of departure for almost all of Anderson's people, from his first published work to his last.

In the Winesburg, Ohio, of Anderson's literary memory and imagination, the wanderers are those who still harbor some vestige of hope—of escape, of life, of possible ultimate fulfillment—and the sojourners are those who for some reason— that of age, of biology, of fear or frustration—have come to the end of a line that stretches far behind them in time, in space, or in psychological torment. But whether each is a wanderer or a sojourner or both, Anderson defines the people of Winesburg as ultimately sharing the same intensely human characteristic, however that characteristic may manifest itself in their lives, their dreams, the ultimate reality of their individual psyches.

In "The Book of the Grotesque" the prefatory story, Anderson defines that characteristic in symbolic terms. This is Anderson's vision of the people of Winesburg as grotesques, each of them distorted psychologically if not physically as well by the thoughts become truths become falsehoods that have burdened their lives and made them what they are. In that sketch Anderson makes clear one fact that all of them share. In the mind of the old writer who observes the people of his world, all of them are in motion, each of them parading through the old man's ageless imagination as each shares with the old man the secret or secrets that have made him or her a grotesque. The writer, the empathetic observer, remains still in his bed as they pass before him in endless procession, and, Anderson notes, "All of the men and women the writer had ever known had become grotesques" in the eye of his imagination.

—David D. Anderson, "Wanderers and Sojurners: Sherwood Anderson and the People of Weinsburg." *MidAmerica* 22 (1995): pp. 89–92.

CLARENCE LINDSAY ON THE SMALL TOWN

[Clarence Lindsay is the author of "A. E. Housman's Silly Lad: The Loss of Romantic Consolation" (1999) and "Consequential Identity in Hemingway's A Farewell to Arms" (1997). In the following excerpt from the article, "I Belong in Little Towns:" Sherwood Anderson's Small Town Post-Modernism," Lindsay discusses the nature of the small town in *Winesburg, Ohio*.]

I begin with a few of Anderson's reflections on staying home, just a few, for two reasons: First, the remarkable formal innovations in *Winesburg, Ohio* can be related to Anderson's relationship to the small town. Those features, among them the most radically experimental and post-modernist in the modernist canon, formally express Anderson's psychological, problematic relationship to his small town origins; the seemingly sympathetic and non-overtly judgmental narrator, the narrator's digressions, the textuality of all relationship, and the related-tale nature of this collection of short stores—are the formal equivalence of certain aspects of the small town. The second reason I start with these manifestations of Anderson's compulsive and often compelling commitment to the Midwest and to the small town is that while it is the source of his genius, it is also, like Murphy's very first move in the chess game in Becket's novel, the cause of all Anderson's subsequent trouble.

Anderson's many comments on the small town convey his distinctive sense of its special qualities. Just as Anderson is a major theorist regarding the Midwest, he is also one of our first intellectual thinkers regarding the complexities of the small town, although I must add that his intellectualism is hidden to some extent, first because he works from a very restricted vocabulary and second because much of the intellectual complexity is conveyed artistically through parables. He comes to the subject frequently, indirectly and directly, throughout the autobiographies and letters. When Anderson had first gone to Chicago acting out the familiar small town drama of escape to the big city, his experience had been typical and disillusioning. Forced to work at hard, physical warehouse labor with hard physical warehouse types, Anderson used the Spanish American War as a way of escaping the demeaning futureless job in Chicago to return, if not triumphantly then at least with a good patriotic excuse, to the town which he had fled only a few years before. In those days it was still customary to raise regiments and other units entirely from a particular town or area, so it was possible to go off to war with friends. The enlisted men were likely the same age and had gone to school together, and the officers were older but from the several social layers of the originating town Anderson comments on this odd feature on several occasions, contrasting it with the subsequent practices of the First World War, ostensibly, but clearly sarcastically, approving of the newer impersonal techniques for waging war. What he has to say about the dynamics among the boys and men in the new regiment reveals the contradictions and tensions of the small town from which sprang his greatest work:

> And so there were, just boys from an Ohio country town, with officers from the same town, in a wood in the South being made into soldiers, and I am much afraid not taking the whole affair too seriously.... The captain of our company had been a janitor of a public building back in Ohio, the first lieutenant was a celery raiser on a small farm near our town and the second lieutenant had been a knife grinder in a cutlery factor. (*A Story Teller's Story* 206)

> As for the officers, well, it was to be admitted that in military affairs they knew more than ourselves, but there the superiority ended. It would be just as well for none of them to attempt to put on too much side when we were drilling or were not on actual military duty. The war would soon be over and after a time we would all be going back home. An officer might conceivably "get away" with some sort of injustice for the moment—but a year from now, when we were all at home again.... did the fool want to take the chance of four or five huskies giving him a beating some night in an alleyway. (*A Story Teller's Story* 206-7)

> They discuss their officers, the position of the officer in relation to his men. "I think it's all right," says a doctor's son. "Ed and Doug are all right. They have to live off by themselves and act as though they were something special, kind of grand and wise and gaudy. It's a kind of bluff, I guess, that has to be kept up only I should think it would be kind of tough on them. I should think they might get t feeling they were something special and get themselves into a mess." (*A Story Teller's Story* 207-8)

There are a fair number of separate and important issues here. In the first passage, Anderson identifies an aspect of the small town sensibility, a suspiciousness toward grandness and overstatement, a habit of "not taking things too seriously." This self-conscious anti-romantic posture is a Herb Shriner or Will Rogers shrewd small town debunking of big city/national pretentious bombast. His subsequent statements suggest, however, something beyond this stereotypical small town refusal to get too revved up over puffery. It's not, as we perhaps might have suspected, a matter of the wholesome goodness of the small town folk who know phoniness when they see it, know falseness because they have not been corrupted, because they are "real." Anderson carefully moves beyond the pastoral sentimentalism. The second and third statements suggest that small town folk have big desires, that they either would or might express the full weight of their selves' imperious desires if only they could "get away with it." But they can't because everyone knows them, because the town is, in a very real sense, still with them, the town who knows who these men really are, who will know the enormous gap between what they might aspire to and what they have come from and will have to return to. James Gatz can't be Jay Gatsby at home in North Dakota. And it's not just that those aspirers would feel uncomfortable or embarrassed being caught out by the home folk when they indulge in their pretenses. It's more than that. It's dangerous. Anderson hints a variation of the "you can't go home again" theme: "If you pretend to be something that you are not, 'put on too much side,' it's really not so much the question of inability to go home but a warning that you had better not." Right alongside the delicate hints of a familiar small town comedy, the robust pastoral lad ("Huskies") justifiably taking down a peg or two someone who's gotten too big for his britches, there is a real violence conveyed in words ("beating") that don't quite fit the more acceptable and comfortable context, a sense of the unjust and disproportionate mob punishment of the one who had dared the "injustice." In the second passage Anderson, rather cleverly, insinuates a real tension between the desire for specialness and "home." All the warm associations in a phrase is pried loose from its normal meanings of nurturing, refuge and pure numinous space by means of that beating, done secretly out of public view in the alleyway.

Anderson, at least in his best work, keeps his heroes at home. For him the small town, home, is where this essential American drama of identity is most intensely felt. It is most intensely felt, first, because it is there that the send of limitations is so at odds with the self's hunger for grandness. All through the autobiographies,

Anderson comments on the peculiar restlessness of the American Midwest, especially of the small town. He refers to the hastiness of the building, the flimsiness of the construction, conveying the sense of impermanence:

> Let us (in fancy) imagine for a moment an American lad walking alone at evening in the streets of an American town.
>
> American towns and in particular American towns of the Middle West [of twenty years ago] were not built for beauty, they were not built to be lived in permanently. A dreadful desire of escape, of physical escape, must have got, like a disease, into our fathers' brains. How they pitched the cities and towns together! What an insanity!....
>
> The lad of our fancy walks in the streets of a town hurriedly thrown together, striving to dream his dreams, and must continue to walk in the midst of such ugliness. The cheap hurried ugly construction of American physical life still goes on and on. The idea of permanent residence has not taken hold on us.

No hint here of any heartland mythologies, no sense of sweet place. In fact, Anderson says again and again that to be an American is to have no sense of place: "No man in America quite expected to stay where he happened to be at the moment. Really it was hardly wort while making the spot express himself." (*A Story Teller's Story* 291)

—Clarence Lindsay, "'I Belong in Little Towns:' Sherwood Anderson's Small Town Post-Modernism." *MidAmerica* XXVI (1999): pp. 79-81; 83-84.

PAUL P. SOMERS, JR. ON NARRATIVE DISTANCE

[Paul P. Somers, Jr. is the author of "Roadtrip to Winesburg" (1998) and "Mike Royko: Midwestern Satirist" (1983). In the following excerpt from his article, "Sherwood Anderson's Mastery of Narrative Distance," Somers discusses narrative distance.]

Sherwood Anderson is known for his stories of adolescence, such as "I Want To Know Why" and "I'm a Fool," in which a young narrator is presented ironically in such a way as to reveal himself without the author seeming to intrude, and, to a lesser extent, for stories such as "The Egg," "The Man Who Became a Woman," and "Death in the Woods," which are told by a mature persona who is more than a merely transparent narrator, but whose state of consciousness is secondary to the action of the story. Often overlooked are the lesser known stories in which Anderson maintains the distinct, ironic distance of his narratives of adolescence, while deftly portraying a complex, sophisticated narrative personality. Jamesian elements are prominent in these stories, rather surprisingly, considering Anderson's professed aversion to Henry James.

In *The Rhetoric of Fiction*, Wayne Booth provides insights into the narrative art which will prove helpful in our examination of this neglected aspect of Sherwood Anderson's achievement. Essential to note is the simple but crucial distinction between the narrator, the "I" of a work, and the "implied image of the artist" who controls him. In the stories "There She Is—She Is Taking Her Bath," "The Yellow Gown," and "The Triumph of a Modern or, Send for the Lawyer," we will see that the narrator is manipulated by the implied author, to the extent that the narrator is a dramatic persona the revelation of whose character is vital to the story.

Elaborating on types of narrative distance, Booth specifies various participants in the narrative process among whom varying degrees of distance may exist: 1) Narrator and implied author. 2) Narrator and characters in the story he tells. 3) Narrator and reader's physical, emotional, etc., norms. 4) Implied author and reader's intellectual, moral, or aesthetic norms. 5) Implied author and other characters. Of these types of distance, he identifies the first, distance between narrator and implied author, as the most useful to criticism. "For lack of better terms, I have called a narrator *reliable* when he speaks for or acts in accordance with the norms of the work (which is to say, the implied author's norms), unreliable when he does not." That is, does the author approve or disapprove of the words and deeds of the persona he has created?

This question of reliability is a very important one to Booth, who points out that Prufrock's description of the evening sky as etherized patient is no description at all to the reader curious about the real weather:

> As unreliability increases, there obviously can come a point at which such transformed information ceases to be useful even in characterization of minds, unless the author retains some method of showing what the facts are from which the speaker's interpretations characteristically diverge.

This is especially important in regards to irony, for the achievement of which the author must provide some reliable clue as to what's fact and what's self-delusion on the part of the narrator. The ultimate validity of Booth's condemnation of unreliable narrators, of the evocation of deranged persona, for example, is beyond the scope of this study, although one is inclined to agree with his stipulation that it's one thing for the author deliberately to confuse the reader, another altogether for him to be confused himself. (...)

Discussing "Authorial Silence," Booth writes of the "'Secret Communion' between author and reader": "The effects of deliberate confusion require a nearly complete union of the narrator and reader in a common endeavour, with the author silent and invisible but implicitly concurring, perhaps even sharing his narrator's plight." Here again, we will see Anderson's skill in manipulating the affections of his reader.

Keeping in mind these concepts of narrative reliability, emotional distance between author and reader, and its corollary, "secret communion between author and reader," let us first consider "There She Is—She Is Taking Her Bath" from *Death in the Woods* (1933). This is the account of John Smith, a New York realtor who suspects his young wife of infidelity. All the information comes from him, and so the reader must piece together the clues to determine whether her unfaithfulness is real or a product of Smith's overactive imagination. The husband is an ineffectual man, who has failed in business and has had to put most of his property in his wife's name. He rides the subway to work because she believes buying an automobile would be an extravagance. We learn from him in the second paragraph that he is unable to decide whether he is "a fool, a man suddenly turned mad, or a man whose honor has really been tampered with...." He is quite disturbed and contemplates confronting his wife with some as yet undisclosed piece of evidence. For several pages he marvels at the "insouciance" of his wife, who seems forever to be taking baths and—he is certain—dreaming of some dapper, unscrupulous "young squirt" with a mustache, and plans revenge against said apparently hypothetical squirt: "I am a small man but I tell you that, once aroused, I will fight" (p. 134).

At last, he shows us the first piece of the puzzle: Seventeen days earlier, he had been coming home from work, worrying whether a Mr. Albright would ask him if he intended to sell the property. Anderson leads us to doubt the competence of Smith, who recalls nothing about any such property. He is so confused, he tells us, that that morning he bumped his head on the bathtub, symbolically perhaps, as he bent to pick up his fallen shaving brush. What had happened is that on that evening he had found in the hallway of his apartment building a perfumed note addressed in a man's bold hand to his wife, Mabel Smith. The note had said "Come to the park on Wednesday when the old goat has gone away. Wait for me on the bench near the animal cages where I met you before" (p. 137).

Walking "boldly" into his own living room, he found there a tall young man with a little mustache, pretending to try to sell a vacuum cleaner to Mrs. Smith. Our hero, however, was not to be deceived. After Mrs. Smith excitedly declared she didn't want to buy the machine, Smith showed the young man out and followed him into the hallway, where he saw another young man descending from the floor above with a similar sweeper.

> It is a pretty slick scheme, this carrying carpet sweepers with them, the young men of this generation have worked out, but we older men are not to have the wool pulled over our eyes. I saw through everything at once. The second young man was a confederate and had been concealed in the hallway in order to warn the first young man of my approach. When I got upstairs, of course, the first young man was pretending to sell my wife a carpet sweeper. Perhaps the second young man had

tapped with the handle of the carpet sweeper on the floor above. Now that I think of that I remember there was a tapping sound (pp. 138–39).

—Paul P. Somers, Jr., "Sherwood Anderson's Mastery of Narrative Distance" *Twentieth Century Literature* 23, no. 1 (February, 1977): pp. 85–87.

"Godliness"

Composed later than many of the other stories in *Winesburg, Ohio*, the genesis of the short story entitled "Godliness" was an abandoned attempt at a novel entitled *Immaturity*, which was itself based on Anderson's experience and observations during a relaxing and enjoyable summer spent at Lake Chateaugay in upstate New York, near the Canadian border. The theme of the book, according to Anderson, was "the terrible immaturity and crudeness of all our lives," and in the course of writing that novel, Anderson says that it was "insane" and absurd, burdened like "a really delicious, garrulous, heavy lame fellow with shaggy eyebrows." That material would be reworked into the four-part short story "Godliness" which made its first appearance in *Winesburg, Ohio* in 1919.

"Godliness" is also unique among the stories that comprise *Winesburg, Ohio* in that it contains four separate tales, a miniature cycle of stories itself, which ends with the flight of a youth from his community, and encompasses the history of four generations. However, partly because of these unique characteristics, "Godliness" has not received favorable reactions until recently. Irving Howe dismissed it as a "failure," Jarvis Thurston gave specific criticism to its "heavy-handed preaching about industrialism," while Richard Abcarian said that the story "veers towards the novelistic" and, in so doing, enervates the power of Jesse Bentley's story by adding, unnecessarily, the story of his daughter, Louise. Nevertheless, some critics, such as James Mellard, have praised the multiple ironies contained within "Godliness." And Rosemary Laughlin sees the relationship between this story and the history of two conflicting influences with the American Protestant experience wherein one is both a tool of God's Providence and the individual's belief in material prosperity as proof that one has joined the ranks of the elect. The problems attending an unattainable spiritual communication and a variety of issues concerning Anderson's notion of the grotesque personality are two important seguays to understanding the four stories that comprise "Godliness."

Part I is the story of Jesse Bentley, the owner and overlord of the Bentley farm. From the very outset, we enter a very peculiar world. The farmhouse, which at first appears to be one structure, is really a bizarre building made up of a "cluster of houses joined together in a rather haphazard manner," with a similarly strange interior that required its inhabitants to move about with great difficulty. "[T]here were always steps to be ascended and descended in passing from one room to another," a place so difficult to maneuver in that the entire personality of the farmhouse itself becomes a manifestation of the grotesque, where the difficulty in moving from one room to another serves as a metaphor for the impossibility of any two people communicating with one another. Furthermore, in addition to a group of elderly inhabitants and hired men, there is Aunt Callie Beebe in charge of housekeeping and her pathetic helper, "a dull-witted girl named Eliza Stoughton." However, having given us a status report on the condition of Jesse Bentley's farm, replete with modern machinery and farming techniques, the narrator takes us back to the story of the Bentley family so that we might better understand Jesse's personality.

As we soon find out, Jesse's ancestors were very poor, but extremely hardworking, relentlessly laboring to clear the land. By the time his father and brothers entered the scene, the hard work had paid off and they were now the owners of the farm, but they absolutely insisted on working at the same strenuous pace. "[T]hey clung to old traditions and worked like driven animals." In a word, the family was obsessed, a characteristic which ultimately becomes a hereditary disease. The Bentleys are representative of Anderson's grotesque types, here devoted to an extreme and unnatural work ethic, so much so that they embody some very negative attributes. "Into their lives came little that was not coarse and brutal and outwardly they were themselves coarse and brutal." And, further, the savage aspect of their individual personalities, "their crude and animal-like" inclinations, is finally taken to its tragic conclusion when Enoch Bentley deals a terrible blow to his father, old Tom Bentley, and then hides in the stable, with the full collusion of his mother, secretly waiting to see if his father would die from his terrible beating.

Later on, when the Civil War brings about a change in the Bentley family's fortunes, and his four other brothers are killed, Jesse is summoned home from his studies. He had left home four years earlier to become a theological scholar, hoping to eventually become a Presbyterian minister. Jesse had always been misunderstood, except by his mother, who had died shortly before his return home. And, now that his admirable plans had been thwarted, he would have to take charge of a large farm, thereby being forced to turn away from the spiritual and intellectual life to which he had been drawn, but destined never to realize. Moreover, Jesse, being slight of build, with "the mouth of a sensitive and determined child," seems very unlikely to succeed with such a enormous responsibility, so much so that the townsfolk are amused by the prospect.

But, contrary to popular opinion, the narrator very precipitously reminds us of the peculiarity of the Bentley family legacy for, despite his dreams of a spiritual life, Jesse is as much a grotesque as his deceased siblings. "Jesse Bentley was a fanatic. He was a man born out of his time and place and for this he suffered and made others suffer. Never did he succeed in getting what he wanted out of life and he did not know what he wanted." And, thus, the sensitive young Jesse becomes a tyrannical overlord who finds respite in his ceaseless and obsessive plans to make the farm increasingly successful. In his insatiable appetite for money and the trappings of prosperity, Jesse proves himself to be every bit as driven as his brothers had been. It is his legacy from which he cannot escape and, tragically, he is neither aware of his own defective character nor the absolute impossibility of ever entering into a spiritual communion with God or minister to the needs of others. He is out of synch and out of touch with both himself and the outside world. Instead, Jesse sees himself as a modern-day Biblical prophet, in love with the sound of his own voice, and is deluded into thinking that God would come down to speak with him directly. "Jesse's mind went back to the men of the Old Testament days who had also owned land and herds.... Being a prayerful man he spoke of the matter aloud to God and the sound of his own words strengthened and fed his eagerness." Eventually, Jesse's self-delusion takes on an even more sinister and fanatical quality, causing him to perceive his fellow Ohio farmers as Philistines and the enemies of God. And so the first part of "Godliness" concludes with Jesse, in his blind pursuit of money and success, calling out to God, wishing for a son to be named David, "'who shall help me to pluck at last all of these lands out of the hands of these Philistines and turn them to Thy service and to the building of Thy kingdom on earth.'"

"Godliness" Part II is the story of Jesse Bentley's grandson, David Hardy of Winesburg, Ohio, who, at the age of twelve, and much to his own detriment, takes up residence at the Bentley farm. It is also the story of David's mother, Louise Bentley, "the girl who came into the world on that night when Jesse ran through the fields crying to God that he be given a son." Louise is now very unhappily married to a banker, Mr. John Hardy of Winesburg. She seems to have inherited the family curse of an impetuous disposition, at one time deliberately setting her house of fire, and, in calmer moments, exhibiting severe depression. Living as a recluse, Louise Bentley's life was shrouded in secrecy, a fact which in itself was productive of many rumors. And, thus, her son David had little chance of living a happy childhood and, even worse, he had no one with whom he could share his fears; which causes him to retreat inwardly. "He had a habit of talking aloud to himself, and early in life a spirit of quiet sadness often took possession of him." Both mother and son are versions of the grotesque.

As a result of his inability to change his terrible home life, David, unwittingly, further complicates his already desperate situation by running away to his grandfather Jesse's farm. Even his journey to a false refuge is fraught with danger. A mere boy of twelve, David sets out on a cloudy evening and soon finds himself caught in a thunderstorm. "Into his mind came the conviction that he was walking and running in some terrible void where no one had ever been before," the point being that there simply is no way he can escape his inherited fate. His mother, with whom he had little contact during the last ten years of his life, has always been inaccessible to him, even when he lived at home. Much to everyone's surprise, Louise Bentley easily acquiesces to Jesse Bentley's insistence that her young son remain with him, stating that the farm "is an atmosphere not corrupted by my presence."

Once he has possession of his grandson, Jesse returns to his delusion of divine power, believing David Hardy to be the son he prayed for and whom God delivered to him, "that at last his prayers had been answered." For a time, it appears to David that his new life in the country is ideal, where he is surrounded by pleasant sounds and the good-natured people who worked for his grandfather. But the serenity of the farm proves to be illusive during a pivotal moment when Jesse suddenly remembers an old nightmare of his in which he saw giants ready to rob him of all the possessions he had so greedily acquired, which obsessive fears bring him to "the edge of insanity." David becomes terrified of the transformation in his grandfather and, prying himself free of Jesse's tight grip, he attempts to run away from him. But, ultimately, David stumbles and Jesse brings him back to the farm, leaving David with the erroneous belief that his perception of his grandfather as a dangerous and deranged man is but a nightmare from which he has awoken.

"Godliness" Part III, which is subtitled "Surrender," continues the story of Louise Bentley, married to a successful banker, Mr. John Hardy of Winesburg. But, before the story begins, the narrator prepares us for a tale of her unhappiness and misfortune, informing the reader that this is to be "a story of misunderstanding." From the outset, Part III also promises to be a dispelling of one of Anderson's major themes, the myth of success in business as a fulfillment of the American dream for both John Hardy and his wife. It would seem that Louise Bentley's life is doomed at the very threshold of attaining a secure place in the world. Further, the narrator also makes it very clear that Louise Bentley's character needs to be seen in a social context, representing the frustration and isolation of women as a result of their being marginalized in a society that has rendered them all but invisible. "Before such women as Louise can be understood and their lives made livable, much will have to be done. Thoughtful books will have to be written and thoughtful lives lived by people about them."

Born of a "delicate and overworked mother" and an impulsive and resentful father, Louise's childhood is fraught with hopelessness, Anderson describes Louise as a "neurotic, one of the race of over-sensitive women that in later days industrialism was to bring in such great numbers into the world." However, the harmful effects of that damaging childhood would seemingly appear to be compensated for when Louise is given the opportunity to live in town with the Hardy family so that she may attend Winesburg High School.

The family patriarch, Mr. Albert Hardy, a successful entrepreneur of buggies and wagons, is a great champion of the benefits to be derived from formal schooling and the reading of books, "an enthusiast on the subject of education." And Albert Hardy is very pleased when he receives numerous accolades from Louise's teachers about how smart and diligent a student she is. But, alas, Albert Hardy's unfortunate blindspot is that he is oblivious to the jealousy he causes when comparing Louise to his two very mediocre daughters, Mary and Harriet. He succeeds in engendering their hostility, and they, in turn, make Louise's home life as miserable as possible, with the result that she becomes increasingly alienated and isolated from the two girls. In fact, Louise's only hope is to befriend Mr. Hardy's son, John, who comes up to her second-floor room every evening carrying an armful of wood for the stove. Indeed, in Louise's narrowly circumscribed world, we are once again given another important facet of Anderson's notion of the "grotesque." Because Louise so desperately longs for the human contact which has so far been denied her, her focus on John assumes an obsessive proportion, which unrealistic expectation will only prove to be a tragic disappointment later on. "She thought in him might be found the quality she had all her life been seeking in people ... that between herself and all the other people in the world, a wall had been built up and that she was living just on the edge of some warm inner circle of life that must be quite open and understandable to others."

Thus, in her blind pursuit of some proffered form of human contact with another person, Louise becomes convinced that John Hardy has been hiding in the garden beneath her window so as to be close to her without her knowing. "She was determined to find him ... to hold him in her arms ... to listen while she told him her thoughts and dreams." Indeed, the poignancy of this fantasy is intensified in two important ways. First, she can only conceive of this romantic encounter taking place in the darkness of her room and, in the midst of admitting so much to herself, she overhears Mary Hardy in the parlor entertaining a gentleman caller. It is also here that she is shown to be utterly naïve about sexual matters. "It seemed to her that by some strange impulse of the gods, a great gift had been brought to Mary Hardy and she could not understanding the older woman's determined protest." And, this naiveté emboldens the timid young Louise to slip a note under John Hardy's door one night, declaring her love for him and asking if he can reciprocate those feelings. "'If you are the one for me I want you to come into the orchard at night and make a noise under my window.'"

Some two or three weeks later, John Hardy finally responds to a now despondent Louise Bentley and, without further ado, the narrator informs us that she and John Hardy have become lovers. But that consummation was not something she desired, but, rather, the result of her desperation to bind the young man to her, "so anxious was she to achieve something else that she made no resistance." And, when Louise tells John that she is pregnant, the young man feels compelled to marry her. But Louise has won nothing as the pregnancy proves to be a ruse designed to force John's hand with the result that she has entered into a relationship which can bring no happiness or spiritual communion. "All during the first year Lousie tried to make her husband understand the vague and intangible hunger ... and that was still unsatisfied." Tragically, when she does give birth to her son, David, she is bitterly disappointed and utterly unable to nurture him from the very moment of his entering her life. "When John Hardy reproached her for her cruelty, she laughed. 'It is a man child and will get what it wants anyway.'" As Judith Atlas has said of the victimization of Anderson's women, "Louise Bentley does not have a woman child and she is given no opportunity to satisfy either her love or her need to be loved. She is clearly one of the female victims of Winesburg whose strength and creativity lead nowhere."

"Godliness" Part IV resumes the horrifying story of David Hardy and his deranged grandfather, Mr. Jesse Bentley, at the point where the narrative ended in Part II. David cannot forget his terrifying vision of Jesse's "religious" fanaticism transforming his grandfather into a predatory monster. Part IV of the narrative is consumed with the fanatically possessed grandfather longing to play the part of the Abraham of Genesis 22 whose love for God was so complete that he was willing to sacrifice his son Isaac. Knowing the outcome of Abraham's story, Jesse is convinced that by demonstrating his willingness to sacrifice a young lamb "born out of season," in place of his grandson David, he will become a true man of God. "If I am fortunate and an angel of God should appear, David will see the beauty and glory of God made manifest to man. It will make a true man of God of him also."

The last part of this story presents an aged Jesse Bentley whose relentless pursuit of money and land holds the same tenacious grip on his way of being as it did when he first assumed command of the Bentley farm. "He was exultant and could not conceal his delight." However, Jesse is not at peace with his prosperity, and resumes his previous attempt to effect a direct communication with God. David, for his part, is now fifteen, and every so often he begins to think about how he must make his own way in the world, but he is not able to sustain this line of self-inquiry. "Thoughts of his coming manhood passed and he was content to be a boy with a boy's impulses."

Nevertheless, whatever tentative peace he may be able to achieve, that sense of well-being is to be forever shattered one Saturday afternoon as Jesse Bentley approaches David and tells him they are to go up into the woods. Indeed, Jesse's peace with himself has likewise been eroded as his obsession with making God take notice of him takes over. "For a long time he had been going about feeling very prayerful and humble.... Now he had decided that like the men whose stories filled the pages of the Bible, he would make a sacrifice to God." However, once the hastily assembled sacrificial site is ready to receive its victim, David has already released the lamb whose feet were bound and the animal has escaped with his own life. In fact, his setting the lamb free becomes a source of strength for David Hardy. It also serves to demonstrate his reverence for the sacredness of life for all living creatures. "There was something in the helplessness of the little animal, held so tightly in his arms that gave him courage." With this newly-discovered courage, David is able to break free from this nightmarish scene, never to be heard from again. And, thus, it is with yet another very real instance of fanaticism that the story ends with a completely abject Jesse Bentley. "'It happened because I was too greedy for glory,' he declared, and would have no more to say in the matter."

"Godliness"

Jesse Bentley is summoned from his studies as a theological scholar to run the family farm. He is obsessed with the notion of meaningful communication with God. He prays for a son named David and is instead delivered a daughter. However, his daughter Louise has a son and she names him David.

Louise Bentley is the unwanted and hapless daughter of Jesse Bentley. She is married to John Hardy, a banker. From an early age Louise sought love and compassion, an obsession that manifests itself in her entrapment of John Hardy.

Aunt Callie Beebe is in charge of housekeeping on the Bentley farm.

Eliza Stoughton is the dull-witted domestic helper of Aunt Callie Beebe.

Old Tom Bentley, Jesse's father is a patriarchal figure who, despite coming to own the farm after much of the hard work had been done, continues to work at a strenuous pace. He is eventually dealt a beating by one of his older sons, Enoch Bentley.

David Hardy is Louise Bentley's and John Hardy's son, he is also Jesse Bentley's grandson. At the age of twelve, he runs away from home to live with his grandfather. During his time with Jesse Bentley, David witnessed his grandfather's frightening transformation into a greed driven religious fanatic.

John Hardy of Winesburg is a banker and the husband of Louise Bentley. He is unable to satisfy Louise's "intangible hunger" for closeness and affection.

Albert Hardy of Winesburg, father of John Hardy, becomes the guardian of the young Louise Bentley when she is afforded the opportunity to live in town and attend school.

Mary and Harriet Hardy are the daughters of Mr. Albert Hardy. They are jealous of Louise when she earns high praise in school and the attention of their father Albert Hardy.

CRITICAL VIEWS ON

"Godliness"

JOSEPH DEWEY ON JESSE BENTLEY

[Joseph Dewey is the author of *Novels from Reagan's America: A New Realism* (1999) and *A Dark Time: The Apocalyptic Temper in the American Novel of the Nuclear Age* (1990). In the following excerpt from his article, "No God in the Sky and No God in Myself: 'Godliness' and Anderson's *Winesburg*," Dewey discusses Jesse Bentley as a wraith.]

Of all the wraiths in Winesburg, none seems lonelier than Jesse Bentley. Alone of Anderson's characters, he seems unable to elicit even the sympathy of his creator. Whereas Anderson delicately balances sympathetic amusement with a most profound admiration for his other grotesques, he seems callously unambivalent toward Jesse. In the raging egocentricity of the Ohio landowner who refashions himself into some Old Testament patriarch while shamelessly indulging gross materialism, Anderson seems to express his generation's bitter condemnation of the new age "love of surfaces," the new "religion of getting on" ("To Waldo Franks" 23). To insert this lengthy lampoon of the Puritan work ethic, Anderson seems to set aside awkwardly not only his artist-hero, George Willard, but also his novel's melancholic ambience, the sense of irresistible yearning for communion that so twists the spirits of his other characters. Examined casually, Jesse does not seem to fit with them. Where they are retiring, he is assertive; where they seem frozen and static, he is a dynamo; where they are lost in self-pity, he crows of his many accomplishments; where they bottle themselves up into tiny chambers, he sees with a vision that encompasses hundreds of acres; where they nurse quiet anxieties to escape Winesburg, he thrusts his roots deeply; where they seem confused and plagued by doubts, he subscribes to a clear, teleological order; where they seem curiously infertile, he begats with Biblical intensity. Indeed, it would seem appropriate that Jesse lives far outside the corporation limits of Winesburg, a suggestion of how removed he is from Anderson's other grotesques.

Yet Anderson takes Jesse far more seriously than he would some throwaway caricature of feverish pietism. Indeed, the tales of Jesse Bentley are by far the longest in the book. In the description of the impulses that drive Jesse, Anderson points out that Jesse is driven half by greediness and half by fear. To understand Jesse's appropriateness, the reader must explore the complexity of these fears rather than the simplicity of the greed. Refusing the harsh caricature of Puritanism that figures in the work of Anderson's contemporaries, among them Dreiser and Lewis, Anderson offers a sensitive reading of the original Puritan vision that accounts not only for the intensity of Jesse Bentley's campaign to tame the Ohio wilderness but also for his place in the ongoing story of the evolution of George Willard.[1]

To understand Jesse Bentley, Anderson cautions early, "we will have to go back to an earlier day" (*Winesburg* 64). Jesse Bentley reflects Anderson's fascination with the New England consciousness[2]; in journals and letters Anderson assessed the Puritan legacy, joining other early century writers who, uneasy over the loneliness implicit in the human condition unrelieved even by speculation about a possible union with some divinity, reviewed the fervor of the original Puritans and their dream of seeking the transfiguration possible in a union with God.[3]

What those Puritans sought (and what Jesse seeks two hundred years later) was confirmation of the self through communion with some greater whole, an awesome union between creation and creator, between the timebound and impotent and the fixed and omnipotent. Yet because the only dignity opened to man was such a restoration of his maimed soul with a divinity that felt no obligation to indicate its attention, the Puritan heritage often reflects anxious lives spent searching for ways to connect with an all-too-distant God, to fight the holy struggle with doubt, despair, and self-insufficiency that often eclipsed the remarkably successful struggle to coax a community from the Massachusetts wastes.

This spiritual hunger felt by Puritans struck Anderson deeply.

Although he emphatically rejected the commercial misappropriation of Puritanism and its corruption into the Victorian "virtues" of sexual repression, dry intellectuality, and material acquisition, he did find use for Puritanism in its expressive hunger for communion, a hunger that so many of his Winesburg characters feel. "To the young man a kind of worship of some power outside himself is essential. One has strength and enthusiasm and wants gods to worship" (*A Story Teller's Story* 164).[4] The question that Jesse poses in the novel is one as old as Plymouth Plantation and as immediate as Winesburg itself with its deathly quiet streets: can the imperfect finite earn the infinite, feel the surety of that outside power? In the tradition of Puritan mysticism, Jesse seeks to be blasted by an excess of light. His raging prayers up and down the Wine Creek Valley capture the desperate (and thoroughly) Puritan condition of man never being at home in however splendid a world he finds or builds on earth. Jesse's neat cluster of houses gives ironic testimony to his homelessness; at heart he feels himself an outcast in a Puritan postlapsarian landscape. In an age of exploding capitalism, Jesse resists heroically the purely material. Although tempted by the success of his unending campaign to create a farm non pareil, he finds nevertheless his possessions ultimately unfulfilling. His farm is critical only as a devotion to God. Absurdly he asserts his role as God's chosen; fearfully in the fury of this assertion, he raises traditional questions of Puritan self-insufficiency but to a universe fearfully silent or, worse, fearsomely empty.

The story of Jesse Bentley, then, is not a parable against relentless acquisition or a lampoon of fanatical faith. It is the story of hunger. Jesse's dilemma is not that he is soulless but that his soul is lean and starved. Any satisfaction he may seem to take in his accumulation of land is undercut by this growing desperation for God to assent to its importance. He can dredge a farm from the swamps, drive farmhands relentlessly, work his wife to an early death, even fashion about his own head an unsteady halo—yet without that recognition, without that communion, he is denied peace. As the Puritans discovered, Jesse finds his God incomprehensible, ominously quiet even at times of greatest need. If, as Perry Miller has suggested, the central drama of the Puritan experiment was the relationship between man and his God, it was often a heartcrushingly one-sided communication.

NOTES

Modern Fiction Studies, Volume 35, Number 2, Summer 1989. Copyright © by Purdue Research Foundation. All rights to reproduction in any form reserved.

1. Although evidence in Anderson's letters and in his memoirs indicates that the story of Jesse Bentley figured prominently in the creation of the tales, critical reactions to the story have ranged from Irving Howe's early dismissal of it to John A. McAleer's sympathetic defense but apparent inability to "fit" the Bentley story into the scheme of George Willard. Ralph Ciancio suggests that of all the characters Jesse does not seem able to elicit Anderson's sympathy. Rosemary Laughlin's brief explication helps readers understand the story but does not make a place for the tale in Anderson's larger work. Of recent criticism, John O'Neill best treats the subject although he suggests only a unity of tone rather than specific thematic ties between Jesse and the rest of the work. He does make a persuasive argument for the relationship between David and George but does not make any such claims for ties between Jesse and George. Indeed, O'Neill dismisses Jesse's hunger for his God as "fundamentally adolescent" (78).

2. Both Anthony Hiller and Norman Pearson look at the ties between Anderson and Puritanism. They suggest that Anderson reacted particularly to the writings of Waldo Franks (*Our America*) and of Van Wyck Brooks (*The Wine of the Puritans*), works that treated the influence of the Puritans in harsh, negative terms.

3. Sacvan Bercovicz analyzes the Puritan notions of the self in the American literary tradition. D. Sebastian's unpublished dissertation presents a summary of the Puritan influence at the time of Anderson, a survey that includes Adams, Robinson, Dreiser, London, Crane, Masters, and Lewis.

4. In the letter to Waldo Franks, Anderson writes, "a curious notion came over me. Is it not likely that when the country was new and men were often alone in the fields and forests they got

a sense of bigness outside themselves that has now been lost? I don't mean the conventional religious thing ... the people, I fancy, had a savagery superior to our own. Mystery whispered in the grass." In *A Story Teller's Story* Anderson records a moment of his own experience when such a tie to Otherness was destroyed, leaving him in a paralysis that recalls Jesse: "There was no God in the sky, no God in myself, no conviction in myself that I had the power to believe in God, and so I merely knelt in the dust in the silence and no words came to my lips" (270).

—Joseph Dewey, "No God in the Sky and No God in Myself: 'Godliness' and Anderson's *Winesburg*," *Modern Fiction Studies*, vol. 35, no. 2 (Summer 1989): pp. 251-53.

ROBERT H. SYKES ON THE IDENTITY OF THE FANATICAL FARMER

[Robert H. Sykes is the author of "A Commentary on Updike's Astronomer" (1971) and "A Source for Mark Twain's Feud" (1967). In the following excerpt from his article, "The Identity of Anderson's Fanatical Farmer," Sykes identifies the character of Jesse Bentley as based on an actual person, Mr. Joseph F. Glidden of DeKalb, Illinois.]

On the several occasions when Sherwood Anderson referred to his Winesburg characters, he disclaimed that any was a specifically identifiable person, insisting instead that they were imaginative figures drawn from many different sources. In a letter to Waldo Frank on November 14, 1916, he said the tales were "studies of people of my hometown" of Clyde, Ohio.[1] But in "A Writer's Conception of Realism," he said, "The book was written in a crowded tenement district of Chicago. The hint for almost every character was taken from my fellow lodgers in a large rooming house."[2] Later he wrote in his *Memoirs*, "I had got the characters of the book everywhere about me, in towns in which I had lived, in the Army, in factories and offices."[3]

At least one of the characters in Winesburg, though, can be

identified as the fictional counterpart of an actual person. The life of Joseph F. Glidden of DeKalb, Illinois, gave Anderson raw material for his portrait of Jesse Bentley in the story "Godliness." (...)

Throughout the story, the details about Jesse dovetail too specifically with the life of Joseph Glidden to be coincidental. Anderson wrote, i.e., "The Bentley family had been in Northern Ohio for several generations before Jesse's time. They came from New York State and took up land when the country was new and land could be had at a low price."[5] Glidden also came from New York at age 33, migrating with his family from Orleans County to DeKalb.[6]

The fictional Jesse and the real-life Glidden were both educated for the ministry before reverting to farming. Of Jesse, Anderson wrote, "At eighteen, he had left home to go to school ... and eventually to become a minister of the Presbyterian Church" (p. 66). Likewise, Joseph Glidden attended Middlebury Academy and then studied "at the seminary at Lima, N.Y."[7]

Two other analogies have to do with their wives and children; each had a wife who died in childbirth, and each was survived by a daughter.[8]

In two places Anderson used the specific number of 600 acres as the size of Jesse Bentley's first farm: "When he came home to take charge of the farm, that had at that time grown to more than 600 acres ..." (p. 66), and "He grew avaricious and was impatient that the farm contained only six hundred acres" (p. 72). In the *Biographical Record of DeKalb County* is the arresting notation about Glidden that, "In the winter after his arrival he purchased six hundred acres of land on Section 22, DeKalb Township, a mile west of the village."[9] He and Anderson's Jesse became land barons of an identical order. "Jesse at night walked beyond his own farm and through the fields of his neighbors and thought that all the land he had traversed should belong to him" (p. 72). Later we find, "The effort he had made to extend his land holdings had been successful and there were few farms in the valley that did not belong to him" (p. 80). Transaction receipts among the Glidden papers in the Archives of Northern Illinois University attest that Glidden ultimately acquired eight farms that originally surrounded his 600 acres.

Anderson differentiates Jesse from his neighbors by the fact that the old man was the only farmer among them to drain his fields. He had built modern barns "and most of the land was drained with carefully laid drain tile" (p. 64). "Great ditches had to be dug and thousands of tile laid. Neighboring farmers shook their heads over the expense" (p. 97). In this respect it is noteworthy that Glidden had a nephew who was a drainage engineer who had come to live with his uncle and drained the Glidden farms into what is now a 40-acre lake on the NIU campus. The Glidden papers there contain receipts for 51 invoices and bills for elbows, stone, brick, and drain tile.

The most convincing detail, however, linking Jesse Bentley with Joseph Glidden is the reference Anderson makes to Jesse's invention, "a machine for the making of fence out of wire" (p. 81). It is for his role in the invention of barbed wire and the invention of the machine to make it that Joseph Glidden is best known to the world. After years of patent litigation, the United States Supreme Court decision on February 29, 1892, established Glidden's original patent. It is important to observe that Anderson did not say he invented barbed wire, but that he said he invented a *machine* for the making of wire fencing. Glidden's patent specifically refers to the machine he invented to hold the spur wires.[10]

NOTES

1. *Letters of Sherwood Anderson*, ed. Howard Mumford Jones and Walter B. Rideout (Boston: Little, Brown and Co., 1953), p. 4.

2. Quoted by Horace Gregory in his Intro. to *The Portable Sherwood Anderson*, rev. ed. (New York: Viking, 1972).

3. *Sherwood Anderson's Memoirs* (New York: Harcourt, Brace and Co., 1942), p. 295.

5. Sherwood Anderson, *Winesburg, Ohio*, ed. Malcolm Cowley (New York: Viking Press, 1975). All citations from "Godliness" are from this edition and hereafter are in parentheses in the text.

6. *Biographical Record of DeKalb County* (Chicago: S. J. Clarke, 1898), p. 600.

7. Ibid.

8. Ibid.

9. Ibid. The Plat Book of DeKalb County of 1892 in the

present township Office of DeKalb shows the original 600 acres.

10. "Barbed Wire—Who Invented It?" *Iron Age*, 117 (June 1926), 1769–1774.

—Robert H. Sykes, "The Identity of Anderson's Fanatical Farmer," *Studies in Short Fiction*, vol. 18, no. 1 (Winter 1981): pp. 79-81.

ROSEMARY M. LAUGHLIN ON THE AMERICAN DREAM

[Rosemary M. Laughlin is the author of "Faces of Power in the Novels of John Fowles" (1972) and "Anne Bradstreet: Poet in Search of Form" (1970). In the following excerpt from her article, "Godliness and the American Dream in Winesburg, Ohio," McLaughlin discusses the characters as aspects of Anderson's "grotesques."]

Though "Godliness" is by far the longest and most structurally complicated tale in the *Winesburg, Ohio* collection, it has received perhaps the least critical attention. When it is mentioned at all it is usually summarily dismissed, somewhat as a grotesque out of step with its fellow grotesques in the cycle of stories. But the story is outstanding precisely because it is brilliantly in step with the other stories in the frame, and with a larger context outside as well. Especially by its style, symbols and characters it is integrally attached to the Winesburg grotesques, while by its structure, themes and mythic elements it is clearly connected with several significant streams of American literary tradition. The smooth interlay of all these elements in a fascinating tale attests to a highly conscious and sophisticated skill on the part of the author, Sherwood Anderson.

I

The grotesques of Winesburg are those who are agonizingly incomplete or unfulfilled, those who have had to suppress their overwhelming desires and needs to love, and, according to the

Writer who collected their stories, those who mistook a myth or falsehood for a truth around which to center their lives. As a result, they express their frustrations or delusions sporadically in eccentric behavior.

There are a number of characters in "Godliness" who fulfill this description. The central character, Jesse Bentley, the "odd sheep" of his family, has taken for truth the belief that material prosperity and rugged individualism are the formula for God's blessings and for mystical communication with Him. His obsession with this belief defeats his spiritual aspirations and ruins the lives of those related to him. By his own admission at the end, his folly alone has brought about the loss of the thing he treasured most, his grandson, David. "It happened because I was too greedy for glory," he declares (p. 102).

Jesse's daughter, Louise Hardy, is a frightening social misfit as the whole town knows. She drives her horse-drawn carriage through the streets like a madwoman, oblivious to whatever is in the way, and hides herself in her room for days at a time, completely ignoring her husband and son. The root of her behavior is misunderstanding. As a child and then as a young girl she craved love and received none. So she withdrew into her studies in a lonely room of the Hardy house where she boarded during the school week. Suddenly "the age-old woman's desire to be possessed" (p. 94) awakens in her when she secretly watches the flirtatious Mary Hardy making love with her beau in the parlor. And so, just as her pioneer ancestors had been impelled by a strange power to shout to the stars at night, Louise is moved by overwhelming desire to throw her arms around a young hired farm hand, and then to write a passionate love note to young John Hardy. John responds, and when the fear of pregnancy that compels them to marry proves false, she feels tricked and becomes an embittered woman. For the rest of her life she festers like an open wound in the atmosphere of her own corrupt presence (p. 78).

Denied of almost any social contacts by their isolation on Jesse's farm, the two Bentley sisters have also become grotesques. But long dormant dreams and desires of love and motherhood are stirred by the coming of the young David to the farm, and they are moved to strange actions. Sherley Bentley sits on the floor beside his bed each night until he falls asleep. "When he became drowsy she became bold and whispered things that he later thought he must have dreamed.... He also grew bold and reaching out his hand stroked the face of the woman on the floor so that she was ecstatically happy. Everyone in the old house became happy after the boy went there" (p. 79). But David can bring only a limited portion of new life for the sisters. They are old and cannot recapture the time or youth that would give them a complete fulfillment.

The symbols Anderson uses in the tale clearly enforce the grotesqueness of the characters, and they are related to symbol patterns in the entire Winesburg cycle. Perhaps the most intriguing of these is the farmhouse itself. It is the first thing Anderson pictures in detail, completely dominating the vague image of the "colorless, soft-voiced lot of old people" sitting on its front porch. It is a strange house, "in reality not one house but a cluster of houses joined together in a rather haphazard manner. Inside the place was full of surprises. One went up steps from the living room into the dining room and there were always steps to be ascended or descended in passing from one room to another" (p. 63).

Though it was not uncommon that a pioneer farmhouse should expand haphazardly as the family grew and needed room, the Bentley home is nevertheless a weird and bizarre hodge-podge. Its maze-like irregularities suggest the patched or twisted lives of its inhabitants, most of whom are brooding old people. Every so often the empty laughter of Elizabeth Stoughton, the half-witted chore girl, echoes through the rooms jarring the ominous silence. Only at mealtimes does the house become alive. Directed by Jesse to jobs and duties, no one has time or occasion for human communication.

The symbolic farmhouse strikes the same note for "Godliness" that the New York room of young Enoch Robinson does in "Loneliness," the room that "was long and narrow like a hallway" (p. 168) and peopled by creatures of his imagination; or as does "the half-decayed veranda of a small frame house that stood near the edge of a ravine" (p. 27), from which Wing Biddlebaum in "Hands" watches the youthful harvesters of Winesburg and thinks of his own decayed life; or as does the empty, stifling, cobwebbed office of Doctor Reefy in "Paper Pills," or the shabby faded rooms of Elizabeth Willard's desolate hotel in "Mother."

—Rosemary M. Laughlin, "Godliness and the American Dream in Winesburg, Ohio," *Twentieth Century Literature*, vol. 13, no. 1 (April 1967): pp. 97-98.

JOHN O'NEILL ON NARRATIVE FUNCTION

[John O'Neill is the author of *Essaying Montaigne: A Study of the Renaissance Institution of Writing and Reading* (2001) and *Freud and the Passions* (1996). In the following excerpt from his article, "Anderson Writ Large: 'Godliness' in *Winesburg, Ohio*," O'Neill discusses the integrative function of this story.]

In language and form, Sherwood Anderson's "Godliness" is simpler, less innovative than most of the other stories in *Winesburg, Ohio*. Perhaps this explains why it has received less attention from the critics. We may consult stories like "Hands" and "Paper Pills" for insight into the experimental features of Anderson's work, aspects which make him an important figure in the development of the American short story and in the emergence of a twentieth century prose style. But when we come to assess all of Anderson's work, not just that which was innovative, it becomes equally important to understand precisely what is taking place in a story like "Godliness," for here the innovative and the traditional, in language and fictional technique, are pretty thoroughly fused, as indeed they were, sometimes bewilderingly so, in Anderson's career.

"Godliness" serves an important integrative function in *Winesburg*. Partly because of the story's length and traditional narrative technique, it reveals in a more thorough and straightforward way the nature of the fanatical, the obsessive and the lonely, as well as other key psychological forces at work throughout the book. Jesse's "fanaticism" is provided with a history, and although the narrator offers us no clinical cause for his condition (since as we shall see, none could exist) that condition has at least fairly well defined stages, a period of evolution arranged for us as a story. In fact, Jesse's fanaticism, like the bitter loneliness of his daughter, and the terror of his grandson, exists as part of a history; in the other stories intense emotion exists more in the form of brilliantly evocative gestures, or objects symbolically freighted with pain or bewilderment. The method of "Godliness," like the method of the biblical stories Anderson alludes to, is that of the exemplary tale, fiction's miniature epic; on the other hand, the method of such stories as "Hands" and "Paper Pills" is that of revelation, Andersonian epiphany, although not so bare of conventional narrative and description as the tales of James Joyce's *Dubliners*.

The tone of "Godliness" further helps to integrate the *Winesburg* tales. The narrator's voice bespeaks Anderson's characteristic attitude throughout: the impressive and finely controlled combination of pity for his people and bewildered, sometimes horrified acknowledgment of the energy encased in their stunted dreams and nightmares. Anderson could, after all, sustain this highly charged, mixed tone, a fact which ought to be remembered when we discuss Faulkner's more spectacular achievement of the same kind in *As I Lay Dying* and his notable failures such as *Intruder in the Dust*. With pity and recognition Anderson creates Jesse Bentley, Louise and David Hardy, and his tone is here similar to, if more emphatic than, that with which he draws Dr. Reefy or Elizabeth Willard. So that in this respect, too, "Godliness" integrates by underlining and simplifying for us an element of crucial importance in most of *Winesburg*.

The characters in "Godliness" focus and reinforce our overall impressions of *Winesburg*, for each is seen to be an amplified and dramatically simplified version of the essential types to which Anderson returns over and over again in *Winesburg* and indeed in the best of his stories outside this collection. The essential relations among the characters here are paradigmatic and hence illustrative and integrative versions of the relations among characters in the other stories.

Jesse Bentley is a "fanatic" who wants God to praise and approve of him. Further, Jesse wants God to guarantee that his craftily acquired wealth will not be sacked by "Philistine" farmers of Northern Ohio. He is a strong man with a warped and arrogant vision to which he, like the Reverend Curtis Hartman and Dr. Parcival, has yoked God, not entirely without a certain weirdly adolescent desire for paternal acceptance from this same God.

Jesse's daughter Louise plays out in the story the role so often given to Anderson's women, from Elizabeth Willard to the old woman of "Death in the Woods": as a young woman Louise wants acceptance, love, and the chance to exploit the fact that she is intelligent (just as Elizabeth wishes to profit from her audacity and even old woman Grimes wants to exploit her one talent, feeding). Hope is denied; desperately the woman, here Louise, offers sex in the hope that what the man wants so much may satisfy her desire for love, survival, or glory. Always, and most explicitly in the case of Louise Hardy, sex is only sex, remarkably ineffective as an instrument, a means, or a symbol. Indeed, Anderson's stories, insofar as they deal with women, are almost always *about* sex—here his critics were correct—but sex treated in anything but a sensational or titillating way. His subject was the failure of sex as instrument, as symbol, as a means of exchange powerful enough to evoke something more than sensation. His women, even more than male adolescents like the hero of "I Want to Know Why," believe with disastrous purity of intent in the symbolical, the instrumental power of sex.

David Hardy, the third major character, plays out, in intense and simplified terms, the experience rendered more subtly through George Willard in the other stories. Thus David, no less than Louise and Jesse, is exploited by Anderson to amplify one of the book's essential roles. (Throughout *Winesburg* one of Anderson's key strategies is such amplification, the sudden absurd or pathetic enlarging of a gesture, a feeling even an object or character which, in ordinary perspective, would be normal, banal. Hence, "Godliness" stands in relation to the other *Winesburg* tales as Enoch Robinson's room, Elizabeth Willard's theatrical makeup, and Dr. Parcival's "Let peace brood over this carcass" stand in relation to other details in these stories.) David is first of all of tremendous importance to Jesse. He is the instrument by which security and peace and vindication are to be achieved. The various "grotesques" in the other stories attach a similar if usually unmentioned significance upon George

call and a promise: after manifesting himself to the patriarch and talking personally with him, God says, "Here now is my covenant with you; you shall become the father of a multitude of nations.... I will give to you and to your descendants after you the land you are living in, the whole land of Canaan, to own in perpetuity, and I will be your God" (Genesis 17:1–8). Abraham's response to God and the covenant is simple, yet profound: "Here I am." Jesse Bentley takes, the ancient promise of Canaan as his own, "that as the true servant of God the entire stretch of country through which he had walked should have come into his possession" (Anderson 54).

But, at the same time, and very much unlike Abraham whose faith in God and the covenant does not waver, Jesse becomes convinced that all the other Ohio farmers around him are Philistines trying to wrest the promised land away from him, and he begins to fear the arrival of a Goliath who could defeat his holy mission (55). In this fear, Jesse Bentley convolutes the biblical narratives obviously, for now he is re-enacting the role of ancient Israel's first king, Saul, whose army faced the Philistines and who himself feared he might have to fight the Philistine champion (I Samuel 17:11). And so, as Jesse Bentley's wife lies in bed in the throes of childbirth, he cries out to God for a champion of his own, a son to be called David, who will help him "to pluck at last all of these lands out of the hands of the Philistines and turn them to Thy service and to the building of Thy kingdom on earth" (55). But this too differs from the original biblical story of Jesse; for his family, like Abraham and the other patriarchs, is called by God (I Samuel 16:3). The biblical David becomes a champion by default, drawn into battle with Goliath only when he takes a meal to his brothers (I Samuel 17:12–54). In the biblical narratives, a call always precedes response. Jesse Bentley, in contrast, cries out in search of a call, hoping to draw God's attention to him: "Here I am."

—Thomas Wetzel, "'Beyond Human Understanding': Confusion and the Call in Winesburg, Ohio," *Midamerica* 23 (1996): pp. 11-14.

"Death in the Woods"

"Death in the Woods," which takes its name from the title of Anderson's collection of short stories (*Death in the Woods*), was published in 1933. Though *Death in the Woods* is Anderson's last group of short stories, it is also his least known collection, in part because his publisher, Horace Liveright, went bankrupt before the volume was to be published. Nevertheless, Anderson was determined to make this collection his best group of short stories, and spent a great deal of time and energy in rewriting and perfecting the story. Yet, despite his laboring over this volume, *Death in the Woods* was not well received at the time. The story of a lonely and impoverished old woman who suffered in silence her entire life while serving her husband and son, Anderson considered "Death in the Woods" his crowning achievement within the genre of the short story.

There are several compelling reasons for Anderson's devotion and painstaking efforts in this story. First, the old woman who dies in the woods is one of Anderson's grotesques, one of the "nameless ones" who is condemned to abject silence and anonymity. In a word, she belongs to a type, as do her husband and son. "All country and small-town people have seen such old women, but no one knows much about them." She has been exploited her entire life, first by a brutal German farmer to whom she is bound, a man who rapes her and then threatens to kill her if she tells, and later by a husband and son, who are both associated with criminal activity and unethical behavior. "The husband and son were a tough lot. Although the son was but twenty-one, he had already served a term in jail. It was whispered about that the woman's husband stole horses and ran them off to some other country." Indeed, the family surname of Grimes is strongly suggestive of the evil inherent in their characterization. Second, the tale is told by an adult narrator who cannot escape the adolescent memory of seeing such an old and sickly woman in the woods who suffered the same fate—a woman whom he remembers having "come into town past our house one summer and fall when I was a young boy and was sick with what was called inflammatory rheumatism." The narrator feels "impelled to try to tell the simple story over again." Indeed, his recollection of the scene is likened to "music heard from far off" and this theme of an underlying message, which is always present, albeit difficult to discern. It is also important to see that the direction towards which the narrative flows is, in one sense, towards a clear and audible recognition of a message. That message is the spiritual meaning of the woman's life and comes to fruition at the end of the story with the narrator stating that "even after her death [she] continued feeding animal life," a reference to the bag of bones and meat she was carrying home, which the dogs consume after her death. It is equally important to recognize that the dogs which encircle her diminutive body lying in the snow are far more honorable than her husband or son could ever be. Not only do they show respect for her person by never harming her body, they also check to be sure that she is deceased before they avail themselves of the sack of food she was carrying. As the narrator tells us, there is an instinctive recognition by the dogs that their role is to serve mankind and that it is because of this role that they have been elevated above the wolves from whom they have evolved. "'Now we are no longer wolves. We are dogs, the servants of men. Keep alive, man! When man dies we become wolves again.'"

With respect to the narrator, his compulsion to retell the story at first seems to be the recounting of his sexual awakening, as he describes how he and his brother had gone into the woods to view the body. "One of the men turned her over in the snow," he recalls, "and I saw everything. My whole body trembled.... None of us had ever seen a woman's body before. It may have been the snow, clinging to the frozen flesh that made it look so white and lovely...." But the now adult narrator understandings that what he experienced that day was far more than a sexual initiation. The woman's death, he realizes, had so completed and complemented her life that it had a beauty of its own. She had been a feeder of animal life during her entire existence—cows, pigs, chickens, horses, men and dogs—and she had died as she had lived, carrying a sack of food. Her death is not terrible or frightening, but somehow appropriate, in essence, a silent celebration of her life. "A thing so complete has its own beauty."

"Death in the Woods"

Old Woman, Mrs. Grimes (originally called Ma Marvin in Anderson's earlier version "Death in the Forest"), is a nameless and voiceless victim of society's treatment of women, including the abuse and neglect she endures from her husband and son. Her role in life is to be a feeder of all living things, "horses, cows, pigs, dogs [and] men."

Jake Grimes is compelled to marry Mrs. Grimes by an equally brutal German farmer for whom Jake worked. A dishonest and thieving man who is rumored to steal horses, Jake has all but forsaken his wife, leaving her impoverished and alone.

Young Mr. Grimes is tough and brutal like his father—at twenty-one he has already served a jail term. He has an affair with a woman whom he brings home one summer and the two order the old woman around as if she were their slave.

"Death in the Woods"

CLARE COLQUITT ON THE READER AS VOYEUR

[Clare Colquitt is a contributing editor of *A Forward Glance: New Essays on Edith Wharton* (1999) and the author of "Edith Wharton as Propagandist and Novelist: Competing Visions of 'The Great War'" (1999). In the following excerpt from her article, "The Reader as Voyeur: Complicitous Transformations in 'Death in the Woods,'" Colquitt discusses the voyeuristic role of the reader.]

Like most writers, Sherwood Anderson was vitally concerned with the workings of the imagination and the creation of art. For Anderson, these concerns were also inextricably linked to questions of personal salvation. In letters to his son John, himself a painter, Anderson asserted that "The object of art ... is to save yourself": "Self is the grand disease. It is what we are all trying to lose" (*Letters* 166, 167). Given Anderson's faith in the redemptive possibilities of art, it is not surprising that the writer frequently compared "literary [and nonliterary] composition to the experience of pregnancy and deliverance, and also to the poles of maleness and femaleness in life" (*Letters* xv). One letter composed three years before the author's death well illustrates Anderson's understanding of the problematic nature of such "deliverance":

> The trouble with the creative impulse ... is that it tends to lift you up too high into a sort of drunkenness and then drop you down too low. There is an artist lurking in every man. The high spots for the creative man come too seldom. He is like a woman who has been put on her back and made pregnant, but even after he gets the seed in him, he has to carry it a long time before anything comes out. (Letters 414)

If, as Anderson claims, "There is an artist lurking in every man," so, also, did the writer believe that there is a woman "lurking" in every artist. Indeed, the image of the male artist whose "lurking" burden is the female within is depicted repeatedly in the correspondence, perhaps nowhere more explicitly than in a letter Anderson sent late in life to his mother-in-law, Laura Lou Copenhaver: "There is a woman hidden away in every artist. Like the woman he becomes pregnant. He gives birth. When the children of his world are spoken of rudely or, through stupidity, not understood, there is a hurt that anyone who has not been pregnant, who has not given birth, will never understand" (*Letters* 428).[1]

The assumptions "hidden away" within such assertions are easily gleaned from letters in which Anderson frankly acknowledges his "old-fashioned"[2] views about men and women. In another letter to his son John, Anderson admitted, "I do not believe that, at bottom, they [women] have the least interest in art. What their lover gives to work they cannot get" (*Letters* 187). As a result, the writer held that the sole "high spot" available for women to experience in life is childbirth. To be sure, Anderson understood that the biological impulse also moves man,[3] but, as he makes clear in letters to his male friends, the love of woman "isn't enough for an eager man": "No woman could ever be in herself what we want or think we want" (*Letters* 168, 324). Thus, whereas woman's destiny is circumscribed by biology, man's destiny transcends the purely physical and finds consummate expression only in the creation of art. (...)

The "tru[ly] male" quality of Anderson's artistic imagination and of his polarized worldview is forcefully represented in his short stories and novels, as well as in his letters and memoirs. Indeed, to speak of woman's destiny in the context of Anderson's fiction is to call to mind what is undoubtedly one of the master storyteller's most disturbing tales, "Death in the Woods." Written at the "peak of his [creative] powers" (Howe 160), "Death in the Woods" has provoked a varied critical response, ranging from interpretations that see the tale much as Anderson claims he did, as a biological allegory depicting woman as feeder, to more recent interpretations that focus less upon the plight of the old farm woman and more upon the narrative consciousness that constructs her story. This shift of focus has led several critics to conclude that "Death in the Woods" is "a story about the creation of a story" (Joselyn 256; see also Robinson), hence Anderson's many attempts to unveil the mechanics of the creative process through the workings of the tale's narrative center, an older man who looks back to one scene from his childhood out of which he will spin his yarn.[4] (...)

Having been thus directed toward the ostensible subject of the story, the reader soon finds that the interpretative process is effectively impeded by obtrusive references the narrator makes concerning his own past. Indeed, in the opening section of "Death in the Woods," the reader learns almost as much about the narrator's childhood as about the plight of old country women. Interestingly, the narrator's allusions to his past closely resemble the boyhood recollections set forth in Anderson's memoirs; yet, despite the similarities that seem to link the storyteller with his tale, Anderson himself "persistent[ly]" interpreted the narrative of Mrs. Jake Grimes in thematic, not autobiographical, terms:

> In a note for an anthology Anderson wrote that "the theme of the story is the persistent animal hunger of man. There are these women who spend their whole lives, rather dumbly, feeding this hunger.... [The story's aim] is to retain the sense of mystery in life while showing at the same time, at what cost our ordinary animal hungers are sometimes fed." (Howe 165)

Anderson's reading is a superb illustration of what John Berger calls critical mystification—"the process of explaining away what might otherwise be evident" (15–16)—for as Irving Howe noted more than thirty years ago, this interpretation is "apt, though limited.... Anderson could hardly have failed to notice that the story may be read as an oblique rendering of what he believed to be the central facts about his mother's life: a silent drudgery in the service of men, an obliteration of self to feed their 'persistent animal hunger,' and then death" (166). Regardless of the limits of Anderson's analysis, one fact is clear: Anderson, like his narrator, is trying to steer critics of "Death in the Woods" away from the realm of history—from the varying records of a writer's conflicted relationship with his mother—to the hallowed domain of myth. Having fastened upon a presumably "safe" and unalterable interpretation of his story, Anderson thereby avoids public confrontation with painful memories of his childhood.

NOTES

1. One of Anderson's most illuminating apologies for his "children" appears in *A Story Teller's Story*, where the artist/mother records his discomfort at once having to listen to a speaker who "praised [him] as a writer but spoke slightingly of the figures that lived in the tales [*Winesburg, Ohio*]":

> Could the man not understand that he was doing a quite unpermissible thing? As well go into the bedroom of a woman during her lying-in and say to her—"You are no doubt a very nice woman but the child to which you have just given birth is a little monster and will be hanged." Surely any man can understand that, to such a one, it might be permitted to speak at any length regarding her own failings as a woman but—if the child live—surely this other thing must not be done. "It must not be condemned for the failings of the mother," I thought shivering with fright. (93–94)

For similar imagery, see also letters to Charles Bockler, Norman Holmes Pearson, and Gilbert Wilson (17 February 1931, 242–243; after 13 September 1937, 387–388; 12 October 1937, 390).

2. The term is Anderson's and comes from a letter to Roger Sergel in which the writer explains why "the modern factory" has affected men and women differently:

> I dare say I [am] an old-fashioned male. I do not think that men and women are alike or that they react to life in the same way. I know that saying this often annoys some women, but still I stand my ground. I do not believe that women employees have been hurt by the modern factory as men have. It is possible for the woman to create in her own person in the flesh, and it is not possible for men. It seems to me that to be is as important as to do. Basically, I do believe that the robbing of man of big craft, his touch with tools and materials by

modern industry does tend to make him spiritually impotent. I believe that spiritual impotence eventually leads to a physical impotence. This belief is basic in me. The darkness is a darkness of the soul. (Letters 377)

3. Anderson's awareness of his own physical needs is well suggested in his correspondence. As he wrote Roger and Ruth Sergel, "I've never been able to work without a woman to love. Perhaps I'm cruel. They are earth and sky and warmth and light to me. I'm like an Irish peasant, taking potatoes out of the ground. I live by the woman I love. I take from her" (*Letters* 245). As I will argue in my paper, the narrator of "Death in the Woods" is similarly parasitic, for, like the other men particularized in the story, the artist/narrator also feeds upon the hapless Mrs. Grimes.

4. Many critics have observed the frequency with which Anderson portrays artists in his work. William V. Miller, for example, asserts that "the most important character type in Anderson's stories is the artist. His stories are filled not only with painters and writers but also with potential artists, story-tellers like May Edgley in 'Unused'; and what may be called the 'artistic impulse' is shared by an even wider scope of characters." Although he never discusses "Death in the Woods," Miller's comments on Anderson and his narrator/artists also apply to that story:

[T]he distinctive narrators, whether they be Anderson thinly disguised or separate characters, are actively present in the stories, apparently creating the tale as it progresses and inviting attention to the process through little asides like "I don't know how I learned this" or "you know how it is." Indeed, after we recognize the full dimensions of the role of the artist in Anderson's fiction, rare is the story in which we do not discover elements of this role. (13)

—Clare Colquitt, "The Reader as Voyeur: Complicitous Transformations in 'Death in the Woods,'" *Modern Fiction Studies*, vol. 32, no. 2 (Summer 1986): pp. 175-77; 179.

[Mary Anne Ferguson is the author of "The Female Novel of Development and the Myth of Psyche" (1983) and "*My Antonia* in Women's Studies: Pioneer Women and Men-The Myth and the Reality" (1989). In the following excerpt from her article, "Sherwood Anderson's *Death in the Woods*: Toward a New Realism," Ferguson discusses the change in the narrator's persona.]

Anderson's cockiness about having achieved his goal of "real integrity" in *Death in the Woods* suggests that the volume may represent a new departure for him. I find in the volume a movement away from a persona seeking the meaning of life in "the preternatural or archetypal," a passive observer upon whom reality impinges itself, toward a persona who shares the life he observes and locates the center of reality outside himself. The change in the persona is associated in the volume with a change in attitude toward women and toward death.

The story "Death in the Woods" is the first in the volume; "Brother Death" is the last, and Anderson indicates that this arrangement was his intention. Obviously the volume is unified by the theme of death; but it is not death alone. As he had elsewhere, Anderson links the topics death and woman. Of the sixteen stories in the volume, five deal with the death of a woman and its effect upon a male character. In "Death in the Woods" the male narrator is a stranger to the woman whose death is an episode in his development. In three other stories—"The Return," "Another Wife," and "The Flood"—the focus is on a widower trying to find a substitute for his dead wife. The narrator of "In a Strange Town" flees his wife and home in order to recover from the depression he felt upon the death of a young woman student; he consoles himself by meditating upon the meaning of life for a widow he sees at a railroad station in a funeral party. These stories reflect the conviction which led Anderson to publish *Perhaps Women* in spite of his dissatisfaction with its form, his sense "that modern man is losing his ability to retain his manhood in the face of the modern way of utilizing the machine and that what hope there is for him lies in women." (...)

Even for the adults in "A Death in the Forest," the old woman's death is not deeply significant. It occurs as an interruption to the town's happy preparation for Christmas and enjoyment of winter, "crowds of boys ... shouting and laughing" as they jump on and are thrown from bobsleds on Main Street. The first sentence of the story announces the death bluntly: "It was December and snowing when Mrs. Ike Marvin—we knew her as Ma Marvin—died in the little hollow in the center of Grimes' woods, about two miles south of our Ohio town." The next two paragraphs personify the town: the return home of a few girls rich enough to have been away at boarding school and of Ben Lewis makes the narrator feel "one's town putting its nose up in the air like a fine pointer dog" on "a day to remember." The day is memorable because of the effect on the townsmen of the news of Mrs. Marvin's death: all activity in the town ceases, and the narrator recalls in detail what many of the townsmen were doing as "things went bang then, like putting a light out in a room." He recalls the bustle as the news is shouted by two young hunters who run down Main Street, figures remembered as "not quite human ... more like Gods." The sudden cessation of activity is accompanied by a change in the weather as the townspeople, including "even women who had no babies to look after," went in a group to the scene. The old woman's life and the manner of her death, "Just as plain as though there had been an eyewitness to her death there to tell the tale," are very briefly summarized. The narrator remembers the "white, half frozen little old figure, pitched a little forward," and the "pack of big ugly dogs"; he imagines "the stillness of death coming softly, night and the cold," but comments "My boy's mind couldn't grasp it then" and goes on to give details of Ben Lewis' participation in moving the body and handing him the coat to hold. In this version it is the boy as part of the town, indeed, the town itself which is the center of the story.

In the three published versions of the story the old woman's death and her life become the central memory of the adult narrator and the story becomes his attempt to perceive its true significance. The final version published in 1933 intensifies the mystical and mythical nature of the experience and its effect upon the narrator as a boy. All three of these versions omit any reference to Ben Lewis and his coat. The immediate impact of the death scene on the narrator and his brother is its function as sexual initiation for them: "She did not look old, lying there in that light, frozen and still. One of the men turned her over in the snow and I saw everything. My body trembled ... and so did my brother's. It might have been the cold. Neither of us had ever seen a woman's body before" (20).

But before this scene the story of the old woman's life as a bound girl, as brutalized wife and mother, as a person totally isolated from human contact, has been amply told; the boy's previous impressions of her during a summer when he had observed her when he was idled by sickness, make his interest in her believable; his final view of her as a "feeder of animals" is made convincing when he presents it as arrived at "slowly, long afterward" (22).

Anderson gains credibility for the narrator in the published versions by carefully detailing his relationship to the old woman. An omniscient narrator first describes the old woman's trip to town on the fatal day as one of many such trips viewed "one summer and fall" by the boy. Her actions are presented as those habitual to "such old women" often seen by "all country and small-town people" but seldom understood by anyone. The use of the present tense to describe habitual action and of the conditional in verbs like "may own" and "might spend" is interrupted in the second paragraph by a specific statement about the boy's distaste for liver; now he becomes the central consciousness but the use of the habitual present continues. "The old farm woman got some liver..." is inconspicuous in the midst of the habitual present; it prepares the reader to believe the narrator's assertion that he had often observed the old woman. Continued shifts between the habitual present and the specific preterite are reinforced by apparently casual explanations of the narrator's knowledge both of the woman's past and of the day of her death. Such observations as "she got into my thoughts," "I remembered afterwards," "I later knew all about it. It must have stuck in my mind from small town tales, heard when I loitered about where men talked," augmented by conversational tags like "You see," "Well," "Maybe," and rhetorical questions like "then what would she do?", subtly establish the tone of oral narration, of a tale being told. This tone not only achieves suspension of disbelief but imparts to the old woman's story the aura of myth. The detailed narrative of her death becomes part of a larger story; the sense of strangeness Anderson felt in the Illinois forest is communicated through dwelling on the dogs' return to their primordial origin as wolves, their memory of civilization. and perhaps their fear of death expressed in their interrupting their circlings to come close to the old woman, who had stopped to rest against a tree trunk beside a clearing. Further details about the dogs' tearing into the old woman's bag of supplies and tearing off her dress "clear to the hips" prepare for the denouement when the narrator and his brother "saw everything" and perceived the body of the old woman as that of a slender young girl.

—Mary Anne Ferguson, "Sherwood Anderson's *Death in the Woods*: Toward a New Realism," *Midamerica* 7 (1980): pp. 74; 78-80.

SISTER MARY JOSELYN, O.S.B. ON ARTISTIC DIMENSIONS

[Sister Mary Joselyn, O.S.B. is the author of "Some Artistic Dimensions of Sherwood Anderson's 'Death in the Woods.'" In the following excerpt from her article, Sister Mary Joselyn discusses the power of the inherent poetry within the narrative structure.]

An appreciative reader of the modern short narrative marvels at Anderson's skill in this story—the "circling," resonating effect created by the several retellings of the events, the deft but strong and pointed ironies thrown off as it were in passing, a time scheme intricate in the extreme yet managed in a relaxed and casual-seeming style, above all the unerring movement back and forth between the mode of ordinary realism and a highly-charged, universalized and poetic vein. It is this characteristic of

"Death in the Woods," no doubt, that prompted Horace Gregory's observation that though its external form is "plainly that of a story, its internal structure is that of poetry; it has the power of saying more than prose is required to say, and saying it in the fewest words."[1] (...)

One of Jon Lawry's chief findings in "'Death in the Woods' and the Artist's Self in Sherwood Anderson"[2] is that a main theme of the story is the creation of the narrator's consciousness as a man and as an artist. Lawry has correctly identified a transformation theme in the story, as has Mary Rohrberger in relating the woman's life to the metamorphosis of Proserpine, Demeter, and Hecate.[3] Yet both readings are incomplete, for, whether or not one accepts the full mythical interpretation, it can be shown that "Death in the Woods" is built upon at least four transformations, which Anderson has interwoven with unparalleled skill. If, for purposes of analysis, Anderson's intricate time scheme is re-structured as straightforward chronology, the outline of the four basic changes of the story immediately becomes clearer. The most obvious of these—and the one that provides the firmest "story line"—concerns the transformation of Mrs. Grimes.

Piece by piece Anderson fills in the picture of the stages of the woman's life. Almost at the end of the story, the narrator refers to Mrs. Grimes's girlhood "at the German's, and before that, when she was a child and before her mother lit out and left her" (p. 542). The girl, the narrator guesses, probably became a "bound girl" of the German farmer because she did not have any father: "You know what I mean" (p. 536). Bound children were often cruelly treated, were "slaves really." At any rate, the farmer's pursuit of the "young, scared" girl, the hatred and suspicion of the farmer's wife, as well as the girl's own inability to resist the rakish Jake Grimes when he appeared led to a situation by which "She got past being shocked early in life" (p. 540). (...)

In the second section of the story Anderson develops in his brilliantly incantatory prose the picture of the woman in her symbolic role as feeder and nourisher of life. As a young girl at the German farmer's, she had spent every moment of the day feeding animals and men, and this work continues and increases after her marriage. Anderson's rhythmic cadences move from simple realism to mnemonic thematic statement: "... things had to be fed. Men had to be fed, and the horses that weren't any good but maybe could be traded off, and the poor thin cow that hadn't given any milk for three months. Horses, cows, pigs, dogs, men" (p. 539). The "feeder" motif remains in the background of all the remaining sections of the story, shading into irony as the maddened dogs tear the food pack from the woman's shoulders after she freezes to death in the snow. Near the conclusion of the narrative, Anderson returns explicitly to the feeder theme as the narrator attempts, however fumblingly, to probe the deeper meaning of the woman's life:

> The woman who died was destined to feed animal life. Anyway, that is all she ever did. She was feeding animal life before she was born, as a child, as a young woman working on the farm of the German, after she married, when she grew old and when she died. She fed animal life in cows, in chickens, in pigs, in horses, in dogs, in men.... On the night when she died she was hurrying homeward, bearing on her body food for animal life. (p. 548)

While the interpretation of the woman's life afforded in the narrator's recapitulation contains truth, it does not exhaust it. For this, another stage in the woman's metamorphosis is necessary.

When a hunter finds the woman's body in the circle of snow around which the dogs have run their ritual chase, it is "frozen stiff ... the shoulders ... so narrow and the body so slight that in death it looked like the body of some charming young girl" (p. 544). (...)

Finally, the narrator presents his own direct view of the scene when the men and the two boys go to the woods. He remembers that "She did not look old, lying there in that light, frozen and still.... It may have been the snow, clinging to the frozen flesh, that made it look so white and lovely, so like marble" (p. 546). Years later, the memory of the picture there in the forest is still vivid to the narrator: "the men standing about, the naked girlish-looking figure, face down in the snow, the tracks made by the running dogs and the clear cold winter sky above" (p. 547). The woman's metamorphosis is complete; she has passed from girl to woman, feeder, and victim, then to the perpetual, "frozen" embodiment of the young girl, caught in "marble." Through the stages of her transformation her meaning—"A thing so complete has its own beauty" (p. 548)—has been dramatically revealed. But other transformations, some not so dramatic and complete, take place in "Death in the Woods," one of the most interesting of them being the change in the narrator himself.

The most circuitous of the narrative threads in the story traces the development of the central consciousness, that of the narrator, itself Lawry has already carefully analyzed the stages in the completion of the man's sense of his self through his telling of the woman's story expressed as a work of art. According to Lawry, "the discovery of the 'I' necessarily involves the artistic expression of that discovery" (p. 307). The "I" is revealed in three stages, as the boy before the woman's body, as the young man facing the circle of dogs in Illinois, and as the older man still holding to his ideal picture of woman. One may question Lawry's apparent conviction of the finality of this transformation; rather it would seem that since the narrator is still mulling over the deepest significance of what he has experienced, he is himself still "in process," his own future promising still further transformations.

NOTES

1. Introduction, *The Portable Sherwood Anderson* (New York, 1949), p. 27. All references to "Death in the Woods" are to this edition, pp. 532–54.

2. *PMLA*, LXXIV (1959), 306–311.

3. "The Man, The Boy, and The Myth in Sherwood Anderson's 'Death in the Woods,'" *Midcontinent American Studies Journal*, III (Fall 1962), 48–54.

> —Sister Mary Joselyn, O.S.B "Some Artistic Demensions of Sherwood Anderson's 'Death in the Woods.'" *Studies in Short Fiction*, vol. IV, no. 3 (Spring 1967): pp. 252-55.

THOMAS E. KENNEDY ON FICTION AS ITS OWN SUBJECT

[Thomas E. Kennedy is the author of *Robert Coover: A Study of the Short Fiction* (1992) and *Andre Dubus: A Study of the Short Fiction* (1988). In the following excerpt from his article, Kennedy discusses fiction as a subject.]

The terms "metafiction" and "self-reflexive fiction" have been used to denote fiction's deliberately self-conscious employment of technique to bolster the deteriorated equipment of more conventional methods with which the art is concealed. (...)

Conventional plot and linear story are cast aside as hopeless simplifications of the existential experience, or else they are consciously toyed with, manipulated, poked and pinched to squeeze new life from them.

Some readers and writers balk at this sort of experiment or innovation as gimmicky and decadent. They point to Aristotle's classic statement that in the greatest art, the art is least visible. During the decade of debate about this between the mid-sixties and mid-seventies, serious fiction lost many readers to subgenres working more strictly with verisimilitude—most notably the spy genre. Many readers saw these developments in fiction as an abandonment of people and events as subject in favor of excessively self-conscious concerns with technique, language, perception, imagination. Instead of portraits, the reader was offered patterns, deliberate ambiguity, discontinuity, gleefully ironic absurdities. Authors defied the master, James, to poke about visibly, demonstratively, distractingly within the guts of their own fictions.

Yet a dimension more profound than the merely technical is involved in the realm of such exploration—the use of fiction as its own metaphor of self-creation, where the process of the fiction is the ultimate existential expression toward which it progresses. In other words, the fiction-making process is used as a metaphor for the self-creation of human identity. This aspect is central to the theme of both stories to be discussed here.

The idea is not new and certainly was not born in the sixties, although the discussions of that decade may have helped to negotiate some obstacles to the understanding of this aspect of metafiction.

Sophisticated fiction wants a sophisticated reader, and some art takes decades to be comprehended. Elements of this fictional technique are as old as literature itself—found in Gilgamesh, Homer, Virgil, Chaucer, Boccaccio, Shakespeare, Coleridge; the fully developed technique has been in use for more than half a century. Even Nick Carraway was a first-person creative narrator, composing Jay Gatsby consciously before our eyes as Jay himself shaped an identity which grew to an embodiment of the national fiction to be known as the American Dream. Sherwood Anderson, fifty years ago, after nearly a decade of trial and error on it, created a splendid example of the genre which was still being misread by Anderson scholars as recently as 1974. Such misreadings seem to result from a confusion about the borders separating literature from life. An interesting example can be seen in the decision taken by Lionel Trilling for his 1967 anthology *The Experience of Literature* to eliminate the prefatory note to Coleridge's "Kubla Khan, A Vision in a Dream, A Fragment" because "the researches of the American scholar, Professor Elisabeth Schneider, have brought the literal truth [of that prefatory note] into serious question; they suggest that these circumstances of composition [as reported in the prefatory note] were as much the product of the poet's imagination as the poem itself."[1] (...)

The fiction writer tells lies which lead to truth or to reality, which allow us to slash the extraneous and the film of familiarity from our sight and approach that which is quintessential to our condition. Fiction writers spend long periods of time alone with themselves, looking at their words appear on blank pieces of paper. Little wonder that they begin to become taken by the very processes entailed, by the ways in which their words do their will (or perhaps by the way in which they do the will of their words), and use that confrontation to enhance and further the realization of the creation, or that the sophisticated reader can wander with delight through the halls of mirrors created in the process of confronting the process of fiction. (...)

If within the fiction the narrator tells us he wrote a scene about circling dogs because he actually saw that happen once in the woods in Illinois, the *narrator* or narrative persona is telling us that, and the narrative persona is a mask, fiction. If, in reading the memoirs of the author of that fictional narrator, we learn that the author himself thinks he did see those circling dogs in Illinois, but actually can't be certain for he may only have dreamed them, this is extraliterary. In the metafiction with a first-person creative narrator, what the "I" says is fiction. Any statement of fact by that "I" is, in fact, fiction, a part of the metafiction or self-reflexive fiction. Whether or not it is literally true is irrelevant. All that matters is the role the statement serves in the overall fiction of which it is part.

Fifty years ago, Sherwood Anderson gave us such a fiction, "Death in the Woods,"[9] which, while generally recognized as a story of enduring excellence and beauty, is not always seen as the sophisticated, complex, polished piece of self-reflexive fiction that it is. (...)

Yet precisely these so-called clumsy explanations bring the story to its ultimate climax of expression. That the groping of consciousness of the story's creative narrator was fully intended by Anderson, invented by him to bring his story a further dimension in its fulfillment of an act of "imaginative sympathy" with another human life would seem implicit in the fact that Anderson tried to write the story over a dozen times in as many years, and that the creative narrator does not appear in any of the earlier versions.

A detailed recapitulation of the story might help make the point.

The story, about six to seven thousand words long, is arranged in five parts of more or less equal size. The first section begins with a sentence mentioning a particular woman about whom virtually no information is given. Then, instead of beginning to describe *her*, the narrator describes her "type" for the next two paragraphs, even forgetting her for a few sentences to talk about how his family had sometimes eaten free liver from the butcher when he was a child because they were so poor. Then he returns to the woman again, but only for a moment before lapsing into the "type" again: "People drive right down a road and never notice an old woman like that." Finally, in the fourth paragraph, three or four hundred words into the story, he lights in on her and begins to tell about her.

She used to come into town one summer and fall when he was a boy and return home with a heavy sack of food, two or three large, gaunt dogs at her heels. Unspecial, nameless, unknown. But the boy remembers her years later and realizes that what happened to her "is a story."

Her husband was a horse thief, her son an ex-convict. The husband is shunned by the locals, even when he tries to approach them. *His* father had made money from a sawmill, but between the two of them and drink and women, their money and land had dwindled away. He (Jake Grimes) got his wife off a German farmer, a bound girl, parentless, whom the farmer may have been misusing. The narrator tells about this in dramatic detail, in the middle of which he interrupts himself parenthetically to ask, "(I wonder how I know all this. It must have stuck in my mind from small-town tales when I was a boy.)" (This is the first signal, two and a half pages into the story, of the *sub*—or perhaps *superior* theme.) Her duties for the farmer were to feed him and the household and the stock.

NOTES

1. Lionel Trilling, *The Experience of Literature* (New York: Doubleday, 1967), pp. 871–875.
9. Sherwood Anderson, "Death in the Woods," in *Sherwood Anderson's Short Stories*, ed. Maxwell Geismar (New York: Hill & Wang, 1962), pp. 121–132.

> —Thomas E. Kennedy, "Fiction as Its Own Subject: An Essay and Two Examples—Anderson's 'Death in the Woods' and Weaver's 'The Parts of Speech,'" *The Kenyon Review* 9, no. 3 (Summer 1987): pp. 59–60; 64–66.

WILLIAM V. MILLER ON THE ROLE OF THE NARRATOR

[William V. Miller is the author of "Sherwood Anderson's 'Middletown': A Sociology of the Midwestern States" (1992) and "Sexual and Spiritual Ambiguity in 'The

Chrysanthemums'" (1976). In the following excerpt from his article, "Texts, Subtexts and More Texts: Reconstructing the Narrator's Role in Sherwood Anderson's 'Death in the Woods,'" Miller discusses the role of the narrator.]

The nature of Sherwood Anderson's short fiction has elicited much critical attention not only to the "texts" of Anderson's life but also to the "texts" created as his readers encounter the stories. For, on the one hand, Anderson was a very lyrical writer: the range of his character types is narrow, and the most common character type in the stories is largely a projection of his own artistic identity. On the other hand, his oral narrators encourage readers to participate in the creation of the stories. The omniscient author of *Winesburg, Ohio* pleads for poetic assistance in telling the stories, and in a number of the best stories the first-person narrator engages the reader in the epistemological search for meaning with such cries of the heart as "I want to know why." (...)

One of Anderson's texts that has attracted much critical attention is "Death in the Woods." It has the most richly documented genealogy of all of his stories, and no other story more incisively reveals both Anderson's characteristic techniques and his characteristic artistic vision. Yet the studies of this story, even in aggregate, are not totally satisfactory. And recent studies which properly identify the story's chief interpretive crux as the reader's understanding of the narrator's role seem so fixated on Anderson's very real, troubled sexuality that the surface text itself is too often neglected. The intent of this study is to confirm some of these earlier insights about the narrator from a broader textual perspective and to restore the validity of the ostensible text against the claims of certain subtexts. (...)

Knowledge of all of these texts, as well as other statements and biographical information, fortifies the "informed" reader as he engages the chief elements of the final version of "Death in the Woods." Three nexus of real and imagined materials deserve special attention: Anderson's experiences growing up in Camden, then Clyde, Ohio in the last quarter of the nineteenth century; the genealogy of Ma Grimes; and the complex role of the dogs in the story.

Just as he stressed his adolescent experiences in the three main autobiographical works and in most of his best stories, Anderson draws on these experiences in "Death in the Woods," but in a somewhat different way. The texture of sensuous, concrete details of his youth in other tales is a chief source of their power; but in revising "Death in the Woods"—for example, in changes from "Death in the Forest" and the *Tar* version—the focus shifts away from the youth's diurnal pursuits and even the experience of discovering Ma Grimes's body toward those additional recollections which are notes toward the composition of Ma Grimes's identity. While the narrator does have childhood memories of eating liver, Grimes's surliness, and the old woman passing their house one "Summer and Fall," much of what the narrator learned about Ma Grimes was discovered in that long, indeterminate period after the death epiphany. This shift in emphasis does move from the boy to the woman; but it should also be noted that while the death scene may be a foundation episode, it does not dominate the narrator's imaginative construct. To insist on the dominance of either the narrator's paralyzing sexual immaturity (Scheick) or his rapist mentality (Colquitt), for example, obscures the legitimacy of dramatizing the artistic process.

More significant to our understanding of the story are the images of Anderson's own father and mother. During the 1920s Anderson's autobiographical and fictive representations of Irwin Anderson appeared to mellow. Earlier portraits such as that of Windy McPherson and Tom Willard in *Winesburg* stress the irresponsibility and exploitation of women which are epitomized in the characterization of Pa Grimes. More to the point, as the biographers have noted, Anderson often distorted the facts about his parents, idealizing his mother and projecting into the father his own uneasiness about relationships with women. Pa Grimes, the quintessential "feeder," is not so much a veiled portrait of his father as the hyperbolic expression of Anderson's own ambivalence about the male role. We recall the ambivalence of Anderson as a youthful voyeur, Lincoln's twin-minded empathy both for the victimized bound girl and for the basically kind farmer who cannot control his lust, and beyond versions of this text, other stories such as "The Untold Lie."

However, the story features Ma Grimes, not her husband, and

energizing her characterization is Anderson's powerful, idealized, guilt-ridden remembrance of Emma Anderson, who died in 1895 when Anderson was eighteen. His descriptions of Emma in *A Story Teller's Story* and in the dedication to *Winesburg, Ohio* romanticize her beyond the factual evidence. Contrary to Anderson's claims that his mother had been a "bound girl" like Ma Grimes and a mysterious beauty of Italian descent, her heritage was German, and these other claims run counter to the specific biographical evidence. Among the documents we are considering, the early "Fred" fragment most specifically links the dead woman with Anderson's perception of his own mother, as Fred, the typical Anderson protagonist, compares the two women and ponders how animality erodes the dream of mothers.

> —William V. Miller, "Texts, Subtexts and More Texts: Reconstructing the Narrator's Role in Sherwood Anderson's 'Death in the Woods,'" *Exploring the Midwestern Literary Imagination*, Marcia Noe, ed., Troy, N.Y.: The Whitston Publishing Company (1993): pp. 86-87 and 89-90.

WILLIAM J. SCHEICK ON THE COMPULSION FOR REPETITION

[William J. Scheick is the author of *Fictional Structure and Ethics : The Turn-of-the-Century English Novel* (1990) and *The Splintering Frame: The Later Fiction of H.G. Wells* (1984). In the following excerpt from his article, "Compulsion Toward Repetition: Sherwood Anderson's 'Death in the Woods,'" Scheick discusses the significance of repetition.]

In spite of its generally recognized excellence, "Death in the Woods" has frequently escaped careful study. It has been read as a story presenting death as inevitable though not terrible,[1] concerning the pathos of a woman's life and the narrator's response to her death,[2] and focusing on the narrator's enlarged consciousness of the human condition.[3] More perceptive is a recent emphasis on the old woman's representation of the

Demeter–Proserpine–Hecate trilogy[4] and on four transform-ations that occur in the account.[5] Most valuable are two essays concentrating on Sherwood Anderson's notions about art as revealed in the story.[6] None of these studies focuses on the narrator in depth. To do so, however, not only indicates that an alleged narrative problem in the story—"a clumsiness in perspective that forces the narrator to offer a weak explanation of how he could have known the precise circumstances of the old woman's death"[7]—is in fact a crucial feature but also reveals hitherto unacknowledged aesthetic features.

On the surface the story seems a simple allegory on feeding. What has not been sufficiently stressed concerning this theme is the narrator's preoccupation with male (and by implication his own) involvement in the recurrent feeding cycle: "things had to be fed. Men had to be fed, and the horses that weren't any good.... Horses, cows, pigs, dogs, men" (pp. 11–12).[8] This view pertains not merely to man's animal hunger for food but, in a disturbing way for the narrator, includes the adult male's hunger for the sexual victimization of women. At one point the narrator revealingly remarks of the old woman: "Thank heaven, she did not have to feed her husband—in a certain way. That hadn't lasted long after their marriage and after the babies came" (p. 10). Throughout the story the narrator symptomatically discloses a fascination with and a repulsion to this aspect of male feeding. He intends, for instance, his description of the scene in which the dogs tear the dead woman's dress "clear to the hips" (p. 17) to parallel directly an earlier episode in her youth when a German farmer "tore her dress open clear down the front" (p. 7), with the ironic difference that "the dogs had not touched her body" (ibid.).

His perception of man's relation to animal feeding, in this double sense, becomes an important factor in assessing the reason why and the manner in which the narrator tells his story, as we shall see. Equally significant is his awareness of a connection between sex and death. Twice in his report of the battle between the German farmer and Grimes for sexual possession of the woman, then "a young thing," the narrator remarks that she was "scared to death" (pp. 5, 7). That this phrase is more than a cliché for him becomes clearer when he relates his first encounter with sex, which occurs in the woods when he sees the dead woman, stripped to the hips: "One of the men turned her over in the snow and I saw everything. My body trembled with some strange mystical feeling" (pp. 20–21). What he experiences and begins to comprehend is more than he can express; *mystical* is the only word he has for it. But as his relation obliquely indicates, he has received a most disturbing impression of the relation between feeding, sex, and death.

In attributing this strange feeling to the weather—"It might have been the cold" (p. 21)—the narrator unconsciously provides a clue to what has happened to him. In one sense during that mystical moment he identifies with the cold dead body, which no longer looks old but as young as his own. Significantly just as the woman had learned "the habit of silence" (p. 9), so, too, he now "kept silent and went to bed early" (p. 22). Furthermore, throughout the story, the product of his long silence, it becomes increasingly clear that the narrator is incorporating the facts (insofar as he has ascertained and imagined them) of the old woman's life into his own experience, with the consequence that he completely identifies with several events in her life. He, too, he tells us, had been circled by dogs one winter night (p. 16).

Whether or not this incident really occurred is less important than that it underscores the narrator's identification with the old woman. However, the reader's suspicion as to its authenticity is aroused by the revelation of another incident paralleling one during the woman's youth: "Things happened. When I was a young man I worked on the farm of a German. The hired-girl was afraid of her employer. The farmer's wife hated her" (p. 22). What he says may be true, however unlikely the coincidence seems; but what is important is the level at which he identifies with the woman, resulting in a story that finally recounts *their* experience rather than merely *hers*.[9] The narrator's capacity for imaginative interpretation is evident in a scene in which Grimes confronts the men of the town: "When he was leaving he turned around and stared at the men. There was a look of defiance in his eyes. 'Well, I have tried to be friendly. You don't want to talk to me....' He did not say anything actually. 'I'd like to bust one of you on the jaw,' was about what his eyes said" (p. 5). Similar interpretation occurs throughout the story whenever the narrator elliptically moves from objective observation of the woman's dilemma to imaginative identification with her thoughts.

As a result of this intense identification, the narrator readily mixes past and present tense in his account. His confusion of tenses represents a suspension of time identical to what occurs during a mystical experience. He cannot pass beyond that frozen mystical moment when he unconsciously identified with the dead woman. His incomprehensible and therefore inarticulate impression of the underlying bond between feeding, sex, and death has proved traumatic for him; and now he remains suspended between the past of the woman's experience and the future of his own destiny as a mature male.

Notes

1. David D. Anderson, *Sherwood Anderson: An Introduction and Interpretation* (New York: Barnes and Noble), p. 131.

2. Rex Burbank, *Sherwood Anderson: Twayne United States Authors Series* (New York: Twayne, 1964), p. 126.

3. Irving Howe, *Sherwood Anderson* (Palo Alto: Stanford University Press, 1966), p. 167.

4. Mary Rohrberger, "The Man, the Boy, and the Myth: Sherwood Anderson's 'Death in the Woods,'" *Midcontinent American Studies Journal*, 3 (Fall 1962), 48–54.

5. Sister Mary Joselyn, "Some Artistic Dimensions of Sherwood Anderson's 'Death in the Woods,'" *Studies in Short Fiction*, 4 (Spring 1967), 252–259.

6. Wilfred L. Guerin, "'Death in the Woods': Sherwood Anderson's 'Cold Pastoral,'" *The CEA Critic*, 30 (May 1968), 4–5; and especially Jon S. Lawry, "'Death in the Woods' and the Artist's Self in Sherwood Anderson," *PMLA*, 74 (June 1959), 306–311.

7. Howe, p. 167.

8. Quotations from the story are from *Death in the Woods and Other Stories* (New York: Liveright, 1933), pp. 3–24.

9. Concerning the story's allegory of Anderson's idea of how the artist works, Lawry explains: "The artist's self is gained only

through imaginative sympathy with other human lives, an act which is, for Anderson, the fundamental premise of art" (p. 308).

—William J. Scheick, "Compulsion Toward Repetition: Sherwood Anderson's 'Death in the Woods,'" *Studies in Short Fiction* 11, no. 2 (Spring 1974): pp. 141-43.

JULES ZANGER ON ANDERSON'S RECREATION OF TRUTH

[Jules Zanger is the author of "Poetry and Political Rhetoric: Bryant's 'The Prairies'" (2000) and "Poe's Endless Voyage: *The Narrative of Arthur Gordon Pym*" (1986). In the following excerpt from his article, "Cold Pastoral: Sherwood Anderson's 'Death in the Woods,'" Zanger discusses Anderson's use of autobiography to recreate truth within the story.]

The familiar myth of Sherwood Anderson as a folk inspired story teller in part results from his own deliberate attempts to make of himself a legendary figure, liberated equally from bourgeois values and from the literary past. It stems also from the homely familiarity of much of the matter of his fiction and from the illusion of artlessness created by the first person voice he often employed. In his short stories especially, Anderson assumed the persona of a literary naif struggling to articulate and shape his own inchoate responses to the familiar mysteries of growing up, of love and loss, and of death in an American small town. The impression of bewildered simplicity communicated by the narrator was contrived by Anderson both as evidence of the narrator's sincerity (where sophistication might be suspect) and as means for establishing a relationship between narrator and reader in which both participate in the drama of discovering the story together. (...)

In writing "Death in the Woods," Anderson re-organized the particulars of his personal and imaginative experience into what were essentially the patterns and concerns of post-war American literary practice: the attempt to understand the self and especially the self as artist, the employment of myth embodied in naturalistic detail, the reliance on symbolism as a means for linking and revealing the public world and the private secret self: all are characteristics of American writing in the twenties and of "Death in the Woods." (...)

The narrator's knowledge of the relationship between this girl and the farmer is both specific and inexplicable until later in the story when he informs the reader: "When I was a young man I worked on the farm of a German. The hired girl was afraid of her employer. The farmer's wife hated her." The scene in the woods where the dogs circle the solitary dying woman which he describes with precise circumstantiality again violates the narrative voice Anderson has established, until he confides: "I knew all about it afterward, when I grew to be a man, because once in a woods in Illinois, on another winter night, I saw a pack of dogs act just like that." Even the trip of Mrs. Grimes into town through the winter snow which the boy could conceivably have witnessed has its origins in the narrator's recollection of "an old woman who used to come into town past our house one summer and fall when I was a young boy and was sick with what was called inflammatory rheumatism." It is in the imagination of the sick, confined child idly watching the road for any occasion of interest that the story of Mrs. Grimes begins. (...)

Like Walt Whitman's "Out of the Cradle Endlessly Rocking," "Death in the Woods" describes the adult artist recalling the childhood experience which culminates in the reminiscence that is the work before the reader. And like that poem, Anderson's story makes that precipitating experience the confrontation of the innocent child by the adult mysteries of death and sexuality: "One of the men turned her over in the snow and I saw everything. My body trembled with some mystical feeling as did my brother's ... Neither of us had ever seen a woman's body before."

The transformation of the child has been accomplished and confirmed by his perception in the nameless woman in the snow of the whole cycle of womanly life: as youthful object of desire, as mother, as crone. The Ohio bound-girl, fought for by her lovers, then mother of children, and finally feeder of beasts and men, became a peculiarly American Muse, a White Goddess whose triple aspect Anderson has domesticated and made familiar. Under the full moon in the white clearing, surrounded by the dark forest and ringed by the frieze of running dogs, she is apotheosized as "a beautiful young woman." Above her, white fragments of clouds are "racing across the little open space among the trees," precisely as the dogs had raced about her body, linking together the earthly and the celestial. Her naked body, "so white and lovely, so like marble," "mystifies" (in an echo of the mystical feeling the boy feels) the crowd of straggling, curious men and boys, silencing them and transforming the return to town into a ceremonial procession. (...)

Though "Death in the Woods" has parallels to Whitman's, "Out of the Cradle Endlessly Rocking," the literary work with which it has the greatest resonance is Keats's Ode. Mrs. Grimes's story as a shaped, created thing is Anderson's "Cold Pastoral" whose completeness expresses a beauty that transcends the particulars of biography or reportage. When he declares. "A thing so complete has its own beauty," we hear an echo of Keats's enigmatic formulization, "Beauty is Truth—Truth Beauty," just as throughout the story we discover teasing parallels to the Ode. The tale of Mrs. Grimes is, in its own grim way, "a leaf-fringed legend," filled with images of field and forest, overwrought, / with forest branches and the trodden weed." The scenes of violence and sexual passion on the German's farm are almost sardonic American versions of the urn's first panel: "What men or gods are these? What maiden loth? / What mad pursuit? What struggle to escape?" When Cleanth Brooks in his essay, "Keats' Sylvan Historian," spoke of the "frozen moment of loveliness" captured by the marble urn, he might have been speaking of the body in the snow, that "still unravished bride of quietness" who, we are told by Anderson's narrator, is "so white and lovely, so like marble." The emptied town and the religious procession of the poem each has its parallel in Anderson's story. Even the story teller's observation, "I had to pick up the details like music heard from far off" possesses a kind of oblique allusiveness to "Heard melodies are sweet, but those unheard / are sweeter."

—Jules Zanger, "Cold Pastoral: Sherwood Anderson's 'Death in the Woods,'" *The Old Northwest*, vol. 15, nos. 1-2 (Spring-Summer 1990): pp. 19; 23-27.

"The Man Who Became a Woman"

"The Man Who Became a Woman," from the volume, *Horses and Men*, published in 1923, is dedicated to Theodore Dreiser, the American novelist who similarly wrote about the myth of the American dream and the consequences of denying the dictates of one's social status. Dreiser is described as a man, "[i]n whose presence I have sometimes had the same refreshed feeling as when in the presence of a thoroughbred horse." In "The Man Who Became a Woman," the crucial scene of which is set amidst the whitewashed remains of animal skeletons which are to be found behind an abandoned small-town slaughterhouse, Anderson writes of a young man forced by social pressure to deny his individuality because the penalties for nonconformity are exacted in moments of horror, here among "the brutality of the racetrack circuit" which he had previously found so romantically alluring.

It is also another story of a youthful lover of horses, one who lived in sympathetic fraternity with these beautiful creatures. Interestingly, this story, considered one of Anderson's best, was never published in a periodical because Anderson took great exception to the criticism leveled at it, namely that it was "sex-obsessed." Nevertheless, the theme of an adolescent's initiation into adulthood notwithstanding, "The Man Who Became a Woman" resists the suggestion of homosexuality implicit in the title as it deals with the two sides of human nature that Anderson is exploring, namely masculine brutality and feminine compassion, both competing for control, or at least some sort of balance within the boy's perspective. Anderson carefully controls the complex structure and execution of the story, much like the young man's walking round and round in circles with his horse, in order to make known and clarify his theme concerning the need to establish sympathetic bonds in a variety of human relationships and its suppression by masculine social values. "To tell the I suppose I got to love Tom Means.... Americans are shy and timid about saying things like that and a man here don't dare own up he loves another man.... It guess they're afraid it may mean something it don't need to at all." Anderson seems to suggest that human beings will never be free because they permit brutality and compassion to clash with each side defined by sexual identity, instead of being allowed to merge into the oneness that makes up a complete person. Indeed, there is a sensitivity on behalf of the narrator which expresses his telling of the tale in a feminine idiom, exemplified when he describes his story as "a knitting."

Finally, with respect to the title of this story, the narrator's transformation in his sexuality is purely symbolic and imaginative, and involves a process of establishing a feminine, sympathetic bond to a horse and, later, a compassionate understanding for the ways in which women are victimized. Herman truly loves his charge, Pick-it-boy, and attributes his beloved horse with a broken heart. "Maybe he had pretty nearly broken his heart trying to get down to the wire in front ... and now everything inside him was quiet and tired, as it was nearly all the time those days in me." Indeed, the love that Herman felt for the horse allows him to experience an intimate relationship. "He was just himself, doing something with a kind of simplicity. That's what Pick-it-boy was like and I got to feeling it in him ... I got inside him in some way I can't explain and he got inside me." A little further on, this intimate connection becomes physical as the narrator describes his pleasure in touching the horse. "I went over to where he stood and began running my hands all over his body, just because I loved the feel of him and as sometimes, to tell the plain truth, I've felt about touching with my hands the body of a woman I've seen and who I thought was lovely too."

Having established this sympathetic relationship with his horse, Herman is now able to understand how women are victimized. Later on, as he remembers his attempt to flee from two big black men, back from a night on the town and thoroughly drunk, who chase him through a dark field, Herman Dudley remembers that he felt like a timid woman about to be overcome by masculine force. "And now I was that woman, or something like her, myself." Indeed, he remembers being so terrified that he could not even scream. "Could it be because at the time I was a woman? It may be that I was too ashamed of having turned into a girl and being afraid of a man to make any sound." But that terror finally reaches a cathartic level with the result that he had finally been purged of his feeling vulnerable and powerless. "It burned all that silly nonsense about being a girl right out of me." The young man has achieved a far more complete masculine identity.

Moreover, in reflecting on this critical adolescent experience, the adult narrator observes a social dimension to this sympathetic bond, saying that it could only be understood by Negroes, who "would understand what I'm trying to talk about now better than any white man ever will. I mean something about men and animals, something between them." In a word, the narrator is associating the sympathetic bond to a feeling that exists when one is vulnerable.

This story is told by an adult narrator, Herman Dudley, looking back on his life as a nineteen-year-old drug clerk in his father's store in Nebraska. After his father dies and his mother sells the store, the narrator moves to Chicago, but soon becomes sick of his lonely existence in the city and, once again, sets out in pursuit of a great adventure, living the life of a tramp, "riding up and down the land on freight trains and trying to see the world," an adolescent dream of a vagabond existence reminiscent of Huck Finn and Tom Sawyer. Nevertheless, similar to the experiences of Huck and Tom, this romantic vision of a carefree life devoid of any parental or societal restrictions, is fraught with danger. "I even did some stealing in lonely towns at night ... but I was in constant terror of being caught." And, thus, as the narrator informs us, he sought employment as a swipe, grooming horses. It is at the stable that he also meets a young man, Tom Means, five years his senior and who has since gone on to become a well-respected writer. Tom Means, who at the time of their meeting aspires "to write the way a well bred horse runs or trots or paces," is also the focal point of this story in which Herman will attempt, unsuccessfully, to explain to himself an incident that had taken place while in his friend's company. Yet, Herman's narrative is punctuated with numerous expressions of hesitancy and compulsion for rephrasing as, for instance, when he begins by trying to link his friend's previous failures with his marital status: "He was then unmarried and had not been successful as a writer. What I mean is he was free and I guess, with him as with me, there was something he liked about the people who hang about a race track" and all the socially marginal types that are attracted to this place. These attempts at clarification appear to be as much for his own sake as well as for the reader's understanding.

Means, is likewise working temporarily as a groom caring for a horse named Lumpy Joe, which is owned by a man named Alfred Kreymborg. Early in the story, Kreymborg encourages them to go into town "to see the girls," but instead they decide to go off into the country. It is also at this point, at the beginning of their adventure, that the narrator admits to loving Tom Means. He admits this knowing that "Americans are shy and timid about saying things like that and a man here don't dare own up if he loves another man" and struggles to tells us of an incident which he is compelled to relate. Herman's difficulty in revealing some dark secret has been magnified in his own mind many years hence, even though he is now married to a woman named Jessie. In the incident, after Herman has suddenly lost contact with Tom Means, he meets and befriends another groom, "a negro swipe named Burt," whom he likes well enough but cannot get as close to as he had with Tom. "But with a negro you couldn't be close friends like you can with another white man," a depressing fact which causes Herman to feel intensely lonely. And, as the drama increases, Herman's loneliness is intensified by the characters that make up the racetrack circuit, characters who we are told "do not go without women."

As we slowly come to learn, the narrator's difficulty has to do with his former inability to relate to the young women who hung around the racetrack. He tells us he was afraid to even make a date with one of the girls. "We probably would have walked around the town and got off together in the dark somewhere," but this remains mere conjecture on the narrator's part. At the same time, Herman expresses a genuine longing for Tom's company. "When Tom was with me that summer the nights were splendid," but after Tom's departure, Herman has repetitive dreams of "seeing women's bodies and women's lips." Burt senses that something is wrong and tries to look out for Herman so that the boss never knows, while we are left with a narrator who is resistant yet committed to finally reveal the details of this traumatic adolescent experience. Left alone one night after all the other swipes are gone, Herman decides to go to town, stopping at a rough bar frequented by coal miners, a saloon which had once been a farmhouse, set amidst a desolate landscape that even frightened the animals. "The horses hated the place, just as we swipes did." While wandering around in the mud and darkness, there is the ever present feeling of impending terror as when we are given a description of some coke ovens which looked "like the teeth of some man-eating giant."

While at this dingy saloon, Herman happens to look into a mirror, "the old cracked looking glass," at the back of the bar, the reflection of which presents an alarming image. Here, he sees a girl's face instead of his own, "a lonesome and scared girl too." Frightened both by the spectacle as well as the dire consequences he could suffer should any of the men know what he had just seen, Herman flees as a fight starts in the bar. During the fight, a big man with heavy boots crushes another man's shoulder—the bones crunching, reminiscent of a slaughterhouse, makes Herman sick at the sight and the sound of this brutality, and he returns to the safe haven of the stables to sleep. "I was so sick at the thought of human beings that night I could have vomited to think of them at all." Later, awakened by two drunken swipes, two liquored-up black men who mistake him for a girl, the narrator takes on a new sexual identity, thinking of a beautiful young princess he had invented, as a means of surviving this rude assault. "And now I was that woman, or something like her, myself." When he manages to escape this terrible fate, "full of terror" of their violent advances, he falls into the skeletal remains of the heads of sheep and cows, all the while wishing to tell the drunken men that he is not a woman, but unable to make a sound. There he hides for the night, recalling that his tremendous fear was so overwhelming that "[i]t burned all that silly nonsense about being a girl right out of me." The next morning he leaves the racetrack life forever. "The last I saw of all that part of my life was Burt."

"The Man Who Became a Woman"

Herman Dudley, the young narrator, is a novice horse groomer responsible for a gelding named "Pick-it-boy." Throughout much of the tales Herman is uncomfortable about his sexual nature.

Tom Means is a temporary groomer caring for a horse named Lumpy Joe. He is also an aspiring writer who befriends Herman Dudley. His imagination inspires Herman.

Owner of Pick-it-boy is a strange and excitable man from Ohio who previously lost a lot of money at the track.

Alfred Kreymborg is the owner of Lumpy Joe.

Jessie Dudley is Herman Dudley's wife.

Burt is a negro swipe and loyal friend of Herman Dudley.

CRITICAL VIEWS ON
"The Man Who Became a Woman"

IRVING HOWE ON THE AURA OF IMPLIED TERROR

[Irving Howe is the author of *William Faulkner: A Critical Study* (1975) and *The American Newness: Culture and Politics in the Age of Emerson* (1986). In the following excerpt from the chapter entitled "The Short Stories," Howe discusses the subtle effects of implied terror in "The Man Who Became a woman."]

The theme of "The Man Who Became a Woman" is much like that of the earlier story, "I Want to Know Why," but to compare the two is to see how the materials of a good story can be reworked into a great one. "The Man Who Became a Woman" is richer in atmospheric texture than the earlier story, it is more certain in technique and consistent in point of view, it benefits greatly from its narrator's distance, and through the most dramatic incident in all of Anderson's fiction it establishes an aura of implicative terror.

Anderson introduces the racetrack milieu with authentic touches possible only to a writer in complete imaginative control of his materials ("when we had got through eating we would go look at our two horses again"). In this atmosphere Herman Dudley meets Tom Means, an educated swipe who hopes to write stories about horses. "To tell the truth I suppose I got to love Tom ... although I wouldn't have dared say so, then." Through this sentence both the adolescent actor and the adult he has since become are concretely placed. The adolescent of the past and the adult of the present are not completely separated, as they never can be; and something of the adolescent's love for horses comes through in the adult's remark about Tom Means's effort to "write the way a well bred horse runs"—"I don't think he has," a statement that is less a judgment of Tom Means's literary ability than an offering of loyalty to the narrator's own youth. This narrator is not secure in his male adulthood, for the story he is trying to tell represents a threat he does not quite know how to cope with. At several points he interrupts his narrative to assure the reader, and himself, that the remembered incident was thoroughly unusual in his life. Each return to his narrative then brings another variation on its theme.

He loves Tom Means; he loves horses; he is fond of Negro swipes; and though he begins to dream of women, he is virginal. Precisely his extreme awareness of the affective values available in horses and men prevents him from moving toward full adult sexuality. When he walks his horse after a race, "I wished he was a girl sometimes or that I was a girl and he was a man."

One cold rainy night he is so overcome with loneliness that he wanders into a nearby mining town. In a saloon he sees his face in a mirror: "It was a girl's face ... a lonesome and scared girl, too." He is afraid that if the men in the saloon see his "girl's face" there will be trouble. But, of course, the men do not notice it, and the only trouble is a brutal brawl that leaves him "sick at the thought of human beings...." Back at the stables, the boy beds down happily in his horse's stall, "running my hands all over his body, just because I loved the feel of him...." But suddenly the stall is invaded by two half-drunk Negroes who mistake him, "my body being pretty white," for a girl. The boy is too terrified to speak—perhaps the Negroes are right. He runs wildly into nearby woods, feeling that "every tree I came close to looked like a man standing there, ready to grab me." The story reaches its grotesque climax when the boy falls across a horse's skeleton near an old slaughterhouse. "And my hands ... had got hold of the cheeks of that dead horse and the bones of his cheeks were cold as ice with the rain washing over them. White bones wrapped around me and white bones in my hand."

Like "I Want to Know Why," this story is based on a contrast between horses and men, but here the action is less dependent on a naive moral polarity of animal goodness and human depravity. The horses and men are not, as in the earlier story, independent agents whose moral qualities are measured by an adolescent observer; they are rather mental referents of the moment in adolescence when psychic needs and moral standards clash. That moment is presented with commanding skill: its meaning is extended by a skein of sexual images (horses, faces, dreams, trees) unconsciously employed by the boy, and its alternation between incident and reverie, with reverie mirroring the persistent power of incident in the narrator's mind, results in a tightening clamp of suspense. But the story's greatest power is released when the boy stumbles over the horse's skeleton, a brilliant bit of gothic symbolism. The horse is, of course, a love object of adolescence and, as the boy falls over its skeleton, his hands clutching the bones that are the color of his own girlish skin, he is actually tripping, in terror and flight, over the death of his adolescent love. But his encounter with the skeleton allows of another, yet congruent, reading: by a simple inversion of color, the "white bones wrapped around me and white bones in my hand," as well as the terror felt by the boy when he is enveloped by these bones, may be seen as referring to a forbidden homosexual fantasy. The diffused love of adolescence has been destroyed, but one strand of it survives—and it is this which prompts the narrator to rehearse his experience.

One of the most beautiful qualities of the story is the way in which the adolescent's natural affection for Negroes is seen ripening into the adult's complex social understanding. (...)

"The Man Who Became a Woman" gains greatly from having an adult narrator who is deeply involved in his own story, for despite his insistence that he is now thoroughly rid of "all that silly nonsense about being a girl" he reveals how persistently, and poignantly, the adult mind struggles to control the memories of adolescence. Herman Dudley may even be, as he insists, a normal man, but to grant this somewhat desperate claim is to record the precariousness and internal ambiguity of adult normality itself. And this, indeed, is the particular achievement of the story, that through a recollection of adolescence it subtly portrays a complex state of adult emotion.

—Irving Howe, "The Short Stories." *Sherwood Anderson.* (New York: William Sloane Associates, 1951): pp. 160-164.

HOWARD S. BABB'S RESPONSE TO IRVING HOWE

[Howard S. Babb is the editor of *Essays in Stylistic Analysis* (1972) and *The Novels of William Golding* (1970). In the following excerpt from his article, "A Reading of Sherwood Anderson's 'The Man Who Became a

Woman,'" Babb identifies a particular rite of passage in the story, the theme of "an integrity of being that youth must experience" in the process of growing up.]

Although almost anyone's list of Sherwood Anderson's successes in fiction would include "The Man Who Became a Woman," this haunting story has provoked less commentary than it deserves. Irving Howe provides the fullest discussion in *Sherwood Anderson*, though the nature of his book prevents him from treating the story in detail, and we may take his interpretation of it as standard. For Howe, "The Man Who Became a Woman" is concerned essentially with homosexuality, showing us an older man not even yet "secure in his male adulthood" who is driven to narrate some extraordinary experiences of his youth: experiences in which "psychic needs and moral standards clash," and which may reveal the youth's "hysteria as a result of accumulated anxieties about his sexual role."[1] In what follows, I shall not be denying that homosexuality is a major motif, but arguing that Anderson is writing about something more: about a particular integrity of being that the youth must experience as a requisite for growing up. To this extent I shall be reversing Howe's emphasis, suggesting that the story centers on the conditions under which the narrator matures, and taking the homosexuality as one instance among others of the narrator's special quality—his openness to the contrarieties of experience. Perhaps some support for this reading inheres in the fact that the teller periodically denies being homosexual in any ordinary sense (e.g., pp. 188, 207, 209):[2] while these denials may be seen as his psychologically necessary effort to shield himself from the truth, they may also be plausibly viewed as indications that the heart of the story's significance lies elsewhere. In any event, the teller himself—when addressing the reader on behalf of the story—insists on its unconventionality: "I'm puzzled you see, just how to make you feel as I felt that night.... I'm not claiming to be able to inform you or to do you any good. I'm just trying to make you understand some things about me" (p. 208). Disclaiming a traditional instructional or ethical aim, he invites us simply to participate in his crucial experience on "that night."

Before recreating the night's events for us, Herman Dudley

has introduced himself as a man now happily married who feels compelled to rehearse his wayward behavior during a period of adolescence. The period begins with his abandoning a conventional small town and then a typical career as a drug clerk for the life of a swipe at a race track, a world whose members—unconventional by normal moral standards—are yet represented as independent, democratic, and honest in personal relations. In this setting Herman finds his perennial loneliness alleviated by Tom Means, a young man whom he supposes he "got to love ... although I wouldn't have dared say so, then" (p. 188). Their friendship is idealized, as is suggested by the purity of their walks in the country and especially by Tom Means's initiation of the narrator into an awareness of the beauty of horses—a point the story makes most resonantly when Tom cries on celebrating what the driver Pop Geers must feel as "he heads a fast one into the stretch," and Herman Dudley "began to blubber" out of sympathy (p. 193). After Tom goes away, Herman takes up with Burt, a Negro swipe, though he soon realizes that they can't be as "close friends" as two white men could, for "There's been too much talk about the difference between whites and blacks and you're both shy" (pp. 194–195). So Herman is left as lonely as ever, a loneliness assuaged only in one moment of fantasy by his sense of identity with the horse he is cooling out. All through this prologue about race track life, the teller is represented as existing, in his innocence and inexperience, outside the conventions of this unconventional world. But what distinguishes him most sharply from his fellows are the fantasies that grip him—the one about his communion with the horse, and the other about a transformation of the natural world—both of which are characterized by his consciousness of being separated from others and by his sudden access to a transnatural experience.

These fantasies prepare for the main action of the story—three hair-raising incidents which occur on "that night"—in that Herman remains possessed throughout the incidents by a new fantasy: that he has changed into a woman. Overcome with loneliness at the track, he goes to a bar, where he first sees himself in the mirror as a young girl, then watches a "cracked" miner brutally beat up a heckler, and finally leaves, "sick at the thought of human beings" (p. 214). After returning to the track to sleep, he is set upon by two half-drunken Negroes, who apparently take him for a woman. Unable to scream, Herman runs away and, in the climactic incident, falls on the skeleton of a horse. These happenings are tied together by several minor details: the same phrases describe the eyes of the miner and of the Negroes; the miner's lips are "thick, like negroes' lips" (p. 210); an image of the slaughter-house is applied to the miner, and the dead horse is lying in "the old slaughter-house field" (p. 224). But the events are interrelated fundamentally through the meaning that emerges.

Significant in the first incident is the number of facts that ally Herman with the brutal miner. For one thing, we have heard Herman react as bitterly to the horrors of industry as the miner himself does when muttering to his child. In the bar, Herman feels that everyone is laughing at him, but they are actually laughing at the miner. Most important, the miner is presumably crazy, while Herman has just imagined himself become a woman. Generally speaking, Herman views the miner with sympathy, though he is appalled at the viciousness the man displays in almost killing his tormentor. The effect of such details is to suggest that Herman contains the miner within himself, so to speak, encompassing the miner's brutality at the same time that he is disgusted by it.

A similar ambivalence marks Herman's encounter with the Negroes, this incident offering a version of love rather than of death. The crucial fact here is his inability to scream, a point he makes several times, as in: "Just why I couldn't I don't know. Could it be because at the time I was a woman, while at the same time I wasn't a woman? It may be that I was too ashamed of having turned into a girl and being afraid of a man to make any sound" (p. 223). By the logic of the last sentence Herman, as a white man become a woman, is "ashamed" of fearing a Negro as lover. But of course Herman is both man and woman, fleeing from what he cannot protest against—his inability to cry out declaring that half of him welcomes what threatens him. And he is associated with the Negroes in other ways through this episode: as an adult narrator, he utters his sympathy for the sexual plight of Negroes in a white community; and as the adolescent running from the Negroes, he keeps implying that he may in fact be pursued by himself rather than by them (p. 222).

The climactic event echoes the first two in its suggestions of death and love, and again it dramatizes the special quality of Herman through the contrarieties that intermingle to make of his experience a totality beyond, or beneath, the conventional. His falling among the bones of a dead horse is represented as an experience of death united with life, of love with death, even of one realm of being merging with another (in the community of man and horse). The language itself attributes an ambivalent sexuality to Herman, allowing him the position of a male while it endows him with a feminine passivity: "I had fallen right in between the ribs of the horse and they seemed to wrap themselves around me close.... White bones wrapped around me and white bones in my hands" (pp. 224–225). Most important, despite being shaken to the core, he still cannot scream—which is to say that he accepts what happens in all its variety.

NOTES

1. *Sherwood Anderson* (New York and Toronto, 1951), pp. 160–164. James Schevill—in *Sherwood Anderson: His Life and Work* (Denver, Colo., 1951), pp. 188–190—also refers to the narrator's homosexuality, but etherealizes it into "the feminine side of a man's nature" and feels that the narrator is concerned with a "question ... central to the understanding of American society: Why is man in this country often so blindly aggressive? Is it because he refuses to value or understand the feminine side of his life?" I sympathize with Schevill's desire to extract some further meaning from the homosexual tendencies portrayed, but I think his reading has the effect of softening them unduly. My own interpretation of the story owes much to discussions with Robert Estrich and Eric Solomon—which is not to saddle them with responsibility for my views.

2. I give page references to and quote from the story as it appears in *Horses and Men* (New York, 1923).

> —Howard S. Babb, "A Reading of Sherwood Anderson's 'The Man Who Became a Woman.'" *PMLA*, vol. LXXX, no. 4, part 1 (September 1965): pp. 432-433.

[Horace Gregory is the author of *Amy Lowell: Portrait of the Poet in Her Time* (1956) and *D.H. Lawrence: Pilgrim of the Apocalypse: A Critical Study* (1957). In the following excerpt from the Introduction to *The Portable Sherwood Anderson*, Gregory discusses the function of the grotesque in "The Man Who Became a Woman."]

It was only when Anderson saw himself as a character that his re-creation of essential truths began to take on the air of remarkable candor; in his posthumously published *Memoirs* he is frankly bored with the chronological progress of events, and is deliberately careless in the naming of dates, as though everything he had to say about himself belonged to a single moment in the past that is called "once upon a time." In all his autobiographical books and sketches, it is the legend of his life that charmed him and charms his readers; his love of wandering, of men and women, of horses, of Midwestern landscapes, of county fairs, of small-town streets and houses, takes on the colors of a reality that is far more convincing than the figure of their author. The real Anderson is in his stories, in George Willard of Winesburg, in "The Man Who Became a Woman," in "I'm a Fool," in Tar Moorehead, and is notably less visible whenever he assumes the personal pronoun "I" in *A Story-Teller's Story* and in his *Memoirs*. (...)

Anderson's ventures into the higher registers of fancy (which make it strange to think of him as a realist, as he was once classified) did not end with *The Triumph of the Egg*—the ventures had actually begun in "Hands," the first of the *Winesburg* stories, and indeed the prelude to *Winesburg* was called "The Book of the Grotesque." As the image, the theme, and the fear of being grotesque matured in Anderson's imagination, some of the most clearly inspired of his stories were possessed by it. The fears of being strange and, similarly, the painful, half-comic experiences of "growing up," pervade the stories and sketches of *Horses and Men*. The book is literally of horses and men, and no American writer of Anderson's generation or any other has caught the colors, the lights and shadows, the spirit of the race track as well as he; the race track is Anderson's milieu quite as the American county fair is, and among those who write of sports, he is in the company of Ring Lardner and Ernest Hemingway. But here also his view of the scene is a characteristic upward glance, the view of country boys in "I'm a Fool" and "The Man Who Became a Woman." The boys are grooms' helpers, "swipes," and they follow the circuit of race-track activities with the same delight with which their younger brothers would try to enter the world of the traveling Wild West show or circus. The influence of George Borrow's attraction to gypsy life is active here, but Anderson translates it wholly into American sights and scenes.

Yet all this is finally only the happy choice of a decor for what he really has to say, and in "The Man Who Became a Woman" what is said touches upon the fears, the mysteries of adolescence—the fear of the boy (now grown to a man) on discovering that he is "strange," is not wholly masculine, and, underlying this, the fear of sterility and death. With a touch as sure as that of D. H. Lawrence, and with none of the mechanical features of overt psychological fiction, Anderson uses, with deceptive simplicity, the scenes in the barroom and the hay-loft, and the incident of the boy's fall, naked, into the shell of bones which was once the carcass of a horse, as the means to tell his story. None of Anderson's stories, with the exception of "Death in the Woods," is a better example of his skill in giving the so-called common experiences of familiar, everyday life, an aura of internal meaning. In this story there is also the fear of Negro laughter, a fear which enters at extended length into two of his later novels, *Dark Laughter* and *Beyond Desire*. In "The Man Who Became a Woman," that particular fear is made more convincing, more appropriate than in the novels; the boy's innocence, his lack of experience, do much to justify his fear, and the fear properly belongs to the immature, the unpoised, the ignorant.

"I'm a Fool" is done with the same turning of light upon common experience—the telling of an awkward, grotesque, foolish lie. Again it is part of the painful experience of growing up, a boyish shrewdness that failed of its desires; it is the image of the concealed, the fatal mistake made by the glib, the young, the unworldly, who parade their candor and innocence wherever they walk and breathe. (...)

The real Anderson of the stories, sketches, and novels

collected in this volume was one who greatly enjoyed life as he found it, but his discovery of it was no easy accomplishment, and the difficulty of this discovery involves his particular genius as a writer. With the writing of the stories in *Winesburg, Ohio*, that discovery had begun, and when the book was published he was a man of forty-three, an age at which too many American writers have left their best years behind them. In Anderson the hidden riches of his personality and art had flowered late, and through them he expressed as few writers can the sensual joys of living on this earth. Much of what he had to say came from these sources, and in his writings the reader shares with him the poignancy of things seen and heard: images of the race track, the sight of moonlight in winter, the stones held in the hand of Hugh McVey, or, in the last pages of *Winesburg, Ohio*, George Willard at the station platform at seven forty-five in the morning stepping on the train. In these scenes the joy of being is almost kinetic, a joy of bodily movement, of seeing things and human beings in transit, freshly and directly, and then moving on. As the unnamed spectator in his own books, Anderson often becomes the charmed and delighted visitor on earth, and the reader shares with him the sense of discovering, under drab exteriors, the strangeness and the physical beauty in what are usually passed by as ordinary things and people.

—Horace Gregory, "Editor's Introduction." *The Portable Sherwood Anderson*, Horace Gregory, ed. (New York: The Viking Press, 1972): pp. 12-13; 24-25; 30.

LONNA M. MALMSHEIMER ON SEXUAL METAPHOR AS SOCIAL CRITICISM

[Lonna M. Malmsheimer is the author of "Daughters of Zion: New England Roots of American Feminism" (1977). In the following excerpt from the article, "Sexual Metaphor and Social Criticism in Anderson's 'The Man Who Became a Woman,'" Malmsheimer discusses sexuality as a metaphor for social criticism.]

In 1965 Howard S. Babb noted that Sherwood Anderson's *The Man Who Became a Woman* had not provoked the critical attention that a story of such quality deserved. A bit more than a decade later that remains true. Prior to Babb's own discussion, only Irving Howe and James Schevill had devoted more than cursory attention to the story. Howe had offered what was essentially a psychoanalytic interpretation of the story while Schevill had made some attempt to link its themes to its social background. Babb took Howe's as the standard reading, dismissed Schevill's as an "ethereal" version of the standard, and tried to shift the focus of criticism to the "conditions under which the narrator matures." His attempt to emphasize the social aspects of the story was important, but he lost sight of his own mark and primarily discussed, though in other and revealing terms, the story's important maturation themes. Yet an approach which lends more weight to the cultural background of the story and to its implicit social comment permits an integration of the valuable insights of both Howe and Schevill and, in supporting Babb's generalization about the complexity of the story, lends some credence to his extravagant claim that the story is good enough to be favorably compared with Conrad's *Heart of Darkness*.

The basic outlines of the story are relatively clear. Herman Dudley, a mature and "happily married" man, reports an experience in youth which still haunts him. The first half of the narrative is a rambling, but pointed, discussion of Herman's past as it pertains to the events of a single night of terror and mental disorder which colors the rest of his life. On that night, Herman "becomes a woman" and is threatened with rape by two drunken black men. He eventually escapes the rape, and, the following morning, leaves the world of horse racing presumably for a better life. The peculiar power of the story derives not from the plot but from the interplay of social and psychological factors which dictate the climactic events and from the narrator's obvious stress as he attempts to report and understand those factors.

Some psychoanalytical observations are certainly in order.

Irving Howe suggests that Herman Dudley suffers from hysteria produced by accumulated anxieties about his sex role. In the context of Howe's discussion it is difficult to judge whether he means to use the term "hysteria" in its popular sense, to designate a kind of excited mental state, or in its clinical sense, to designate a psychoneurotic state recognizable as a medical problem. Whatever the case, there is an abundance of evidence that the clinical use of the word is appropriate. Herman exhibits the syndrome of true hysteria: preceding the climactic night Herman's sleep is frequently disturbed and he exhibits excessive concern about his physical health. He has "no pep," and his total condition affects his work so that his friend Burt must cover for him. A dependent person, Herman has just lost a mentor and authority figure (Tom Means), a loss common in hysterical illness. Herman says, "it wasn't the same way any more and I got into the fix I have described" (p. 197).

At this point Herman shows signs of acute mental illness. For example, he hallucinates:

> It was like this. Sometimes I would be sitting, perhaps under a tree in the late afternoon.... There were always a lot of other men and boys.... I would listen for a time to their talk and then their voices would seem to go far away. The things I was look- ing at would go far away too. Perhaps there would be a tree, not more than a hundred yards away, and it would just come out of the ground and float away like a thistle. It would get smaller and smaller, way off there in the sky, and then suddenly—bang, it would be back where it belonged, in the ground, and I would begin hearing the voices of the men talking again (p. 196).

While cooling the horses, Herman falls into hypnoid states characterized by early stages of dissociation:

> You walk and walk and walk ... and in a queer way you get so you aren't really part of it all.... I guess something in one got to going round and round and round, too. The sun did some- times and the trees and the clouds of dust. I had to think some- times about putting down my feet so they went down in the right place and I didn't get to staggering like a drunken man (pp. 198–99).

In these states Herman is enough removed from reality that he must be reminded to eat. And those around him clearly recognize that he is not well.

The central experiences reported in the story follow logically from Herman's history and consist of two separate but over-lapping hysterical episodes. In the first episode, precipitated by his entrance into a small-town bar, Herman "becomes a woman":

> The point is that the face I saw in the looking glass back of that bar, when I looked up from my glass of whisky that evening, wasn't my own face at all but the face of a woman. It was a girl's face, that's what I mean. That's what it was. It was a girl's face, and a lonesome and scared girl too. She was just a kid at that (p. 207).

Paranoia accompanies this change: Herman thinks the men in the bar are laughing at him; he worries that "if any of these men in here get on to me there's going to be trouble." In the bar, he witnesses the brutal beating of one local coal miner by another, and this event sends him in retreat to the stable.

The second hysterical episode is precipitated by two drunken black men who discover Herman in the loft of the barn and mistake him for the girl he believes himself to be. Herman responds to the threat of rape with hysterical muteness:

> The devil of it was I couldn't say anything, not even a word. Why I couldn't yell out and say "What the hell," and just kid them a little and shoo them out of there I don't know, but I couldn't. I tried and tried so that my throat hurt but I didn't say a word. I just lay there staring at them (p. 220).

Although Herman cannot speak, he escapes the rape in a terror-filled dash, punctuated by a symbolic rebirth. Thereafter, Herman, released from the acute hysteria, sleeps in relative peace. (...)

Most of those who have commented on the story agree that the difficulty in Herman's life situation relates to sex roles. Fears of homosexuality and impotence are cited as major problems.

Babb, who emphasizes the difficulties of maturation, reasserts the significance of the homosexual themes; in fact, he faults Schevill for overly "softening" them. Yet there is strong evidence that homosexuality is not central to Herman's illness. In the first place, Herman, as the adult narrator, reiterates that homosexuality is not an issue; that alone, of course, is insufficient to dismiss the possibility, since his protests could be indicative of the contrary. But Herman's analysis is supported both by the other symptoms of his mental disorder and by the direct intervention of Anderson himself in the single breach of narrative voice in the story. Neither in the dreams nor in the waking fantasies which form a part of Herman's disturbance does he exhibit homosexual tendencies. Virtually all of his sexual fantasies are of women. In terms of actual relationships, only Herman's friendship with Tom Means could be construed as homosexual, but that view is specifically prohibited by Anderson. The break in narrative voice is apparent:

> To tell the truth I suppose I got to love Tom Means, who was five years older than me, although I wouldn't have dared say so, then. Americans are shy and timid about saying things like that and a man here don't dare own up he loves another man, I've found out, and they are afraid to admit such feelings to themselves even. I guess they're afraid it may be taken to mean something it don't need to at all (p. 188).

Here, too, Anderson points directly to the socio-cultural tensions of the story.

Most importantly, however, any interpretation which centers on homosexuality must account for Herman's response to the threatened homosexual rape. Howard Babb reads the hysterical muteness as an indication that Herman is open to the experience. Yet Herman's hysteria does not prevent him from escaping the rape, thus indicating his subconscious desires. Rather Herman's muteness prevents him from identifying himself as male. That, taken along with the sex change he mentally experiences, is the key to his illness. Herman is perfectly willing to accept his biological role as male; in fact he shows considerable eagerness to do just that. He is, instead, unable to accept his role in terms of maleness as socially defined. He refuses to conform to the male stereotypes which are part of his experience. He is indicating not that he is subconsciously homosexual but that he would rather be a woman than accept maleness as it is defined by his available role models, and it is worth examining those role models as they affect Herman.

> —Lonna M. Malmsheimer, "Sexual Metaphor and Social Criticism in Anderson's 'The Man Who Became a Woman.'" *Studies in American Fiction* 7, no. 1 (Spring 1979): pp. 17-21.

WELFORD DUNAWAY TAYLOR ON THE INITIATION RITUAL

[Welford Dunaway Taylor is the author of *Virginia Authors: Past and Present* (1972) and *The Newsprint Mask: The Tradition of the Fictional Journalist in America* (1991). In the following excerpt from the chapter in his book entitled "Expressing the Inexpressible," Taylor discusses the "bizarre initiation ritual" within the story.]

Like the narrator of "I'm A Fool," Herman Dudley in "The Man Who Became A Woman" is an adolescent horse groom who experiences a cruel initiation. At nineteen Herman has "never been with a woman"; but he fantasizes about them by imagining how his ideal girl should look and "at night dreaming about ... seeing women's bodies and women's lips and things...." Too shy to talk to women, he often feels lonely and despondent, and finds the company of horses more congenial than that of men. He recognizes "how mean and low and all balled-up and twisted-up human beings can become ... just because they are human beings and not simple and clear in their minds, and inside themselves, as animals are...." The one being he shares a close rapport with is the horse Pick-it-boy; he says that each understands the other "in some way I can't explain."

One evening at the end of the racing season, when he feels particularly dejected and the image of his ideal woman is especially vivid, he has several drinks in a saloon. Then, peering into a mirror behind the bar, he sees "not [his] own face but the face of a scared young girl."

Although he admits that he has seen himself as a female on several occasions when he was "a young fellow" (the story is narrated at some point in adulthood, when he is happily married), he is stunned by the reflection in the glass. He hears laughter around him, and he imagines that the other men in the bar have seen the same feminine image. However, their laughter is directed at a strange-looking laborer with a crop of red hair that sticks straight up; he enters the bar with a little boy who looks just like him. The man orders a number of drinks in quick succession, muttering meaningless words under his breath all the while. As he does this, a man in the bar begins to imitate him, which brings gales of laughter from the other drinkers. Suddenly the red-haired man grabs Herman Dudley, shoves him against the bar, and tells him to hold on to the little boy. Herman watches as the red-haired man gives the teasing one a sound beating, then grabs up his son and leaves. Herman is left alone at the bar, unnerved both by having seen himself as a woman and at almost having been involved in the fracas.

Herman returns to Pick-it-boy's stall in a heavy rain, half frightened, half dejected. He goes immediately to Pick-it-boy and begins "running my hands over his body, just because I loved the feel of him and as sometimes, to tell the plain truth, I've felt about touching with my hands the body of a woman I've seen and who I thought was lovely too." Calmed by his closeness with the horse, he climbs to the loft above the stall, removes his rain-drenched clothes, and crawls, naked, beneath a stack of horse blankets.

Just after he falls asleep, he is awakened by two black men, "half liquored up," who have seen him climb into the loft and, at a distance, have mistaken his young white body for that of a woman. He is frightened both by the possibility of a homosexual assault and by the fact that their mistaking him for a girl reinforces his earlier fantasy of seeing himself reflected as a female.

He frees himself from the men and, dropping to the horse stall below, flees, still naked, into the rainy night. He runs through a thick wood, bumping into trees that bruise and scrape his body.

Then he stumbles and falls forward. Feeling himself entrapped, he finds "white bones wrapped around [him] and white bones in [his] hands." He has fallen squarely into the skeleton of a horse, lying near a slaughterhouse located not far from the race track. "I seemed to find myself dead with blind terror," he later recalls, "It was a feeling like the finger of God running down your back and burning you clean...."

The stumbling incident is actually a kind of bizarre initiation ritual. The white bones of the skeleton are stark symbols of death—a death of Herman's innocent fantasies of women and a death of his notions that the world of the race track is superior to the world outside. That the ambience of the race track can be cruel and uncaring is further emphasized when he returns to the track after the episode in the forest. He arrives just as daylight breaks and is greeted by the laughter and jeers of the other grooms.

He leaves as soon as he can get dressed. As his black friend Burt hurls curses at the laughing horsemen and defiantly shakes a pitch-fork at them, Herman is "cutting out along the fence through a gate and down the hill and out of the racehorse and tramp life."

—Welford Dunaway Taylor, "Expressing the Inexpressible," *Sherwood Anderson* (New York: Frederick Ungar Publishing Co., 1977): pp. 65-67.

"I Want to Know Why"

From the volume *The Triumph of the Egg*, "I Want to Know Why" was first published in November 1919 in *Smart Set*. In May of that year, after *Winesburg, Ohio* had been published, Anderson had witnessed the Sir Barton win the Kentucky Derby. There are several biographical facts that inform this story. First, during the time he was working on this story, Anderson was feeling increasingly alienated by his advertising work. Furthermore, Chicago at this time had been rocked by race riots, with Anderson sheltering five black acquaintances in his apartment. Second, while as young boy growing up in Clyde, Ohio, Anderson had developed a love for horses at the racetrack and, among the jobs he held during his youth was grooming the horses at the livery stable. Third, Anderson remembered his intoxicated coworker, Ed, bringing home a prostitute to the stable," the memory of which caused him to feel disgust. And, finally, the narrator's revulsion at the trainer's blatant sexuality may have been Anderson's reaction to his own father's adulterous behavior.

Ostensibly a boy's story of a lad who loves horses, yet cannot understand why grown men become involved with such tawdry substitutes as prostitutes instead of pursuing love and beauty. "It's what gave me the fantods.... The women in the house were all ugly mean-looking women, not nice to look at or be near." The story takes place at the racetrack during the late nineteenth-century. "I Want to Know Why" is the opening story in a narrative sequence linked by a common theme in which the characters are basically isolated from each other, and which isolation is further complicated by the fact that they live within an implicit reality that can be neither explained nor clearly delineated. Nevertheless, "I Want to Know Why" is not about a young boy's initiation into manhood but, rather, the poignant expression of one of the most profound human tragedies: the inability to understand contradictory values and emotions in either society or individuals. "It's because Jerry Tillford, who knows what he does, could see a horse like Sunstreak run, and kiss a woman like that the same day."

The narrator's inability to reconcile the contradictory behavior he observes can be seen in several important instances. The first contradiction is a simple and straightforward one in which the narrator observes that a black man, specifically here the black cook Bildad, will not tell on a boy, whereas a white man will. "They won't squeal on you. ... White men will do that, but not a nigger." The second disillusioning event concerns the ill-intentioned prankster, Harry Hellinfinger of Beckersville, a lazy grownup whose mean-spirited joke makes the narrator physically ill. Upon Harry's advice, the narrator, unfortunately, eats half a cigar, trusting Harry's advice that it will stunt his growth and, thereby, enable him to become horse trainer. The contradictions become increasingly complex, the ultimate being the painful disappointment of listening to a man who seemingly had such admirable qualities, who has the ability to appreciate the beauty of horses, can cavort with a common prostitute. The ultimate and definitive contradiction occurs when the narrator observes Jerry Tillford through the window of a brothel kissing a woman who, though superficially beautiful is nevertheless sullied. As the narrator tells us, she was "hard-mouthed and looked a little like the gleding Middlestride, but not clean like him."

The characters in "I Want to Know Why" are beset by feelings of inadequacy and frustration and are a source of the great disappointment to the disillusioned narrator in this story. In a word, they are grotesques. Anderson's style is that of the oral storyteller in its midwestern rhythms and idioms. Perhaps a clue to understanding the implicit and inexplicable reality resides in the very title of this volume, wherein each of the characters possesses an inner shell containing a secret inviolate. The characters here lack someone like George Willard of Winesburg, a man who could listen to them and, thus, are left utterly without the hope of communication. While the story sustains a strong yet undefined sexuality, it nevertheless draws a direct connection between the racetrack culture of horses, men, women, and sexuality.

In this story, horses are treated as distinct characters with human attributes and individual personality traits, and given highly symbolic names—Sunstreak, Middlestride and Strident. Indeed, the horses are given distinct personalities, exhibiting exemplary behavior, and they become the standard by which the narrator can judge human nature in his story. It is clear from the narrator's description of the three horses that they are the only "characters" who are able to consistently maintain a nobility and sense of purpose, unlike their human owners. Moreover, each of three horses, Middlestride, Sunstreak, and Strident also come to represent an individual sexual persona. Middlestride and Sunstreak are both the kind of horse that makes the narrator's "throat hurt to see." Middlestride, a gelding, is "long and looks awkward," while Sunstreak, a stallion, is "nervous and belongs on the biggest farm we've got in our country." Though Sunstreak is a stallion, he is compared to "a girl you think about sometime but never see"; he is also "hard all over and lovely too." Such ambiguous sexuality is a significant theme in the story in which horses are assigned human attributes. Sunstreak's name implies that he is fast, clear, bright and hot; Middlestride's name suggests a slow, muddled, lumbering, tepid horse. One of the prostitutes at the farmhouse is "like the gelding Middlestride, but not clean like him, but with a hard ugly mouth."

In the end, the narrator, despite his revelation of a secret he has harbored for years, is left with the same unanswered question that prompted his narrative. He simply cannot reconcile Jerry Tillford's contradictory behavior. "It gives me the fantods. What did he do it for? I want to know why."

LIST OF CHARACTERS IN
"I Want to Know Why"

The **Narrator** is a sensitive young man who loves thoroughbred horses. He writes this story about an adolescent experience which he hopes to finally understand.

Jerry Tillford is a horse trainer whom the narrator at first worships and later finds morally corrupt.

Bildad Johnson is a cook with a talent for ensuring steady employment by regaling stable men and horse trainers. He proves to be a loyal friend to the narrator and his young friends.

Harry Hellinfinger is a lazy grownup who enjoys playing mean-spirited jokes on the boys. He angers the narrator by advising him to eat half a cigar so that he can stunt his growth and qualify as a rider.

Hanley Turner, Henry Rieback and **Tom Tumberton** are the other three boys from Beckersville, Kentucky who accompany the narrator on an adventure to the Saratoga racetrack.

Henry Rieback's father is a professional gambler who spends most of his time away from home while visiting other racetracks. He is very generous to his son and is always sending Henry presents. Some of the other parents object to Mr. Rieback.

The **Narrator's father** is a lawyer who does not make much money.

Dave Williams, Arthur Mulford and **Merry Myers** are professional gamblers from Louisville and Lexington, Kentucky.

Joe Thompson is a man from the narrator's hometown—he owns a half dozen horses.

"I Want to Know Why"

JAMES ELLIS ON ANDERSON'S FEAR OF SEXUALITY

[James Ellis is the author of "Robert Frost's Four Types of Belief in 'Birches'" (1993) and "The Bawdy Humor of The King's Camelopard or the Royal Nonesuch" (1991). In the following excerpt from this article, "Sherwood Anderson's Fear of Sexuality: Horses, Men and Homosexuality," Ellis discusses Anderson's fear of sexuality in this story.]

Two of Anderson's most complex stories—"The Man Who Became a Woman" and "I Want to Know Why"—treat this mystery [of human sexuality] with great subtlety. Of the two, "The Man Who Became a Woman" is usually considered the superior and more challenging story, but it seems to me that properly understood, "I Want to Know Why" is in equally challenging and complete presentation of human sexuality.

****

Kim Townsend argues persuasively that what Anderson was asking for was a true "men's friendship—not male bonding, nor homosexual relations ... but friendship...." But I would argue that while Anderson did indeed hope to find in male friendship an asexual communication of spirits, some of his best fiction dramatizes his own understanding that sexuality pervades not only the "natural" world of heterosexuality but also stands mysteriously implicit as a threat to the human spirit in male relationships. Anderson successfully portrayed this conflict in two of his most powerful and artistically satisfying stories—"I Want to Know Why" and "The Man Who Became a Woman."

****

In "The Man Who became a Woman" Herman Dudley is a young, unmarried man of 19 working as a groom in Pennsylvania. He is befriended by a young man, also a groom and unmarried, named Tom Means who ambition it is "to write the way a well-bred horse runs or trots or paces"—in other words, to achieve the utmost purity of art in his writing. Tom becomes Herman's mentor in regard to both horses and spiritual aspiration, telling him that "[t]here isn't any man or woman, not even a fellow's mother, as fine as a horse, that is to say a thoroughbred horse."

Tom Means and Herman Dudley, appropriately, are grooms not for stallions—symbols of the sexual triumph of the masculine flesh—but for geldings, like themselves, innocents before the world of male sexuality. Herman says that Tom's talks "started something inside you that went on and on, and your mind played with it like walking about in a strange town and seeing the sights, and you slipped off to sleep and had splendid dreams and woke up in the morning feeling fine." For some time Tom's talks satisfy Herman's desire for spiritual fulfillment. But when Tom Means leaves for another track, Herman is left adrift.

****

Yet, as Herman later discovers, when he becomes physically the girl of his dreams, the result is not spiritual communication but rather an invitation to sexual assault. So it would seem that as much as Anderson sought in man an outlet for love without the sexual, he was aware that the sexual could and would erupt in relationships, whether it be in male-female or male-male relationships.

Anderson's earlier "I Want to Know Why" is a further and in some ways more subtle treatment of the same problem. The story turns on the experience of a young Kentucky boy who has run away from home to follow the faces at Saratoga. There he meets a trainer from his home named Jerry Tillford, who has prepared the stallion Sunstreak for the big race, the Mullford Handicap. Sunstreak's only possible competition in the race is the gelding Middlestride. But on the day of the race, when the horses are being saddled, the boy and Jerry Tillford look into each other's eyes and they both know that Sunstreak will win the race.

The boy, however, has great respect for both horses. As an innocent and an adolescent just turned 15, he himself is to be identified with the gelding Middlestride, but also at his age he is on the verge of manhood and therefore ready for sexual initiation and identification with the stallion Sunstreak. The race is run and Sunstreak wins as the boy and Jerry Tillford had foreseen. That night the boy walks outside of town and finds himself at "a little rummy-looking farmhouse set in a yard." Suddenly Jerry Tillford and other men associated with horse racing drive up. All are drunk and all go into the farmhouse brothel with the exception of Henry Rieback's father, the gambler, whose form of corruption is money rather than the flesh.

****

It is this brothel scene that gives rise to the title of the story, for the boy will discover here the dual nature of the adult: his ability to serve the spiritual by training the thoroughbred and thereby raising the horse's flesh to its animal perfection, but also his seemingly concomitant desire, not just for physical, reproductive sex, but for the sexual as either the erotic or the lubricious.

The boy's anger is intense, of course, because he sees Jerry as having betrayed the spiritual love that had brought them together in their appreciation of Sunstreak. But I would suggest that there are two further reasons for his great anger and that they speak to Anderson's understanding of the limits of platonic love and the force of sexual and physical love. First, if the boy is still to be identified as an innocent with the male gelding Middlestride, we are justified, I think, in recognizing that on the psychological level he is jealous of his female counterpart, the prostitute who "looked a little like the gelding Middlestride, but not clean like him" and that he feels dispossessed in the affections of Jerry Tillford.

Second, while he feels this jealous, he is further angered to the point that he could kill Jerry Tillford, because in Jerry's physical and sexual advances upon the prostitute, he is also—in the sense that the boy is also to be identified with Middlestride, forcing the repugnant demands of physical sexuality upon the boy and his desire for a spiritual relationship. Jerry Tillford's actions, therefore signal to the boy that gelding (innocent) though the boy may be, and spiritual as his and Jerry's relationship may have been) as represented in their shared appreciation of Sunstreak), the nature of the adult male is always to debase that spiritual relationship by the intrusion of the brutishly sexual. For this reason the boy is outraged and demands to know why such a thing can be.

—James Ellis, "Sherwood Anderson's Fear of Sexuality: Horses, Men, and Homosexuality," *Studies in Short Fiction*, vol. 30, no. 4 (1993 Fall): pp. 595-601.

PETER FREESE ON SOCIALIZATION PROCESS AS THEME

[Peter Freese is the author of *Germany and German Thought in American Literature and Cultural Criticism* (1990) and *"America," Dream or Nightmare: Reflections on a Composite Image* (1990). In the following excerpt from this article, "'Rising in the World' and 'I Want to Know Why': The Socialization Process as Theme of the American Short Story," Freese discusses the American esteem for the age of adolescence and Sherwood Anderson's contribution of the "slice-of-life story" punctuated by digressions and temporal inversions, rather than the traditional, chronologically progressive plot.]

Leafing through Erasmus of Rotterdam's *Colloquia* (1522), which went through more than 130 printings and remained in use as a popular textbook for teaching Latin till the eighteenth century, one finds, for example, the dialogue of a youth with a prostitute or the detailed description of the effects of syphilis in the story of a diseased rake's marriage with a sixteen-year-old innocent girl. Such surprising topics make one realize that a collection of texts which today would stand a fair chance of being indexed as harmful to young persons was long esteemed as a useful schoolbook. Obviously, there were times in which legal concepts like the protection of children and young persons and educational notions like developmental appropriateness were unknown, and in which children, adolescents and adults shared the same social realm.[1] Thus it is no wonder that in older literature the childhood and youth of Telemachus, the son of Ulysses, of Parzival, the foolish boy in the forest of Soltane, or of Simplizius, the wretched farmer's son in the war-ridden Spessart village, are only necessary transitional stages which one could not leave out entirely, but which are hardly treated as developmental phases with their own intrinsic value. (...)

The concept of original sin, thought to have been abolished by enlightened man, came back into favour, now less justified theologically than psychologically and backed up by the disillusioning experiences of recent history, and numerous literary works demonstrated how seemingly innocent children embodied the very evil as the helpless victims of which one had liked to pity them. If, for example, one compares J. D. Salinger's *The Catcher in the Rye* (1951) with William Golding's *Lord of the Flies* (1954), one recognizes how starkly Holden Caulfield and Golding's choir boys contrast with each other as the representatives of two diametrically opposed points of view: the former is a Rousseauistic figure who believes that the original innocence and purity of man has been tainted by the corrupting influence of a 'phoney' civilization; the latter degenerate because of their inherent dispositions into bloodthirsty brutes and act out their creator's conviction that "man is a fallen being. He is gripped by original sin."[8]

It is in the context of the tensions hinted at in the above remarks that the depiction of the socialization process in the American short story has to be studied; and first of all it should be stated that it is not the children but the adolescents who attract the main interest. One reason for such a preference is the fact that there is hardly another country in which the age of adolescence is accorded the same esteem and even reverence as in America, of which the British sociologist Geoffrey Gorer says that the years from twelve to twenty-five are looked at as "the chief *raison d'être* of living,"[9] of which Ihab Hassan diagnoses a "neurosis of innocence,"[10] and in which Grace and Fred M. Hechinger find a *Teen-Age Tyranny* established.[11] Another, and more pertinent, reason is the fact that America, as the country in which fathers abdicate their authority and try to be the pals or even the peers of their sons, in which the daily behaviour of politicians testifies to the pervading influence of the boy-man ideology, and in which the slogan 'Don't trust anybody over thirty,' was invented, has always connected the individual developmental phase of adolescence with the collective chance of beginning anew in the virgin land of a continent free of the fetters of history, and has thus linked the promise of individual youth with the national dream known, since James Truslow Adams, as 'the American Dream.' (...)

If one leaves Hawthorne's story with the ironic last sentence "perhaps ... you may rise in the world without the help of your kinsman" still ringing in one's ears, and examines how seventy years later Sherwood Anderson in "I Want to Know Why" (1919) deals with the same predicament one finds several changes. Instead of the chronological narration from a detached omniscient perspective used in "My Kinsman," one now reads the protagonist's personal report which is characterized by repeated digressions and temporal inversions, and instead of a carefully arranged plot story continuously progressing from exposition to denouement, one faces an abruptly beginning and seemingly incomplete narrative of the new type which Anderson helped to introduce into American literature and which is commonly known as the slice-of-life story. The degree of individualization and introspection has grown considerably, not least under the influence of Freudian psychoanalysis, and also the medium of narration has changed, in the course of America's gaining of her intellectual independence, from the elevated diction of east-coast literature orientating itself by British standards to a genuinely American vernacular derived from the oral tradition of frontier tall-talk; the problems, however, have remained the same. A nameless sixteen-year-old narrator-protagonist tries to give an account of a certain experience he had about a year before, and his disorderly narration, which time and again shies away from the real issue, reveals that he has not yet come to terms with this experience and thus becomes a formal pendant of his bewilderment and his attempt at autotherapy at the same time. The boy is driven by a passion for thoroughbred horses which is an expression of his attempt to escape from an increasingly complicated everyday life into the pastoral microcosm of the race tracks as well as an unconscious expression of his diffuse adolescent sexuality—he compares Sunstreak, his favourite horse, with "a girl you think about sometimes but never see"[27] and would like to kiss it. Thus he runs away with some friends from his little hometown in Kentucky and hitchhikes his way to Saratoga, New York, to watch Sunstreak perform in the decisive race. Sunstreak wins, and in the fulfilling moment of victory the boy's enthusiastic admiration for its trainer Jerry Tillford blossoms into unrestrained love. However, in the evening of the same day the boy follows his idol and sees him squander the very look he had directed at the glorious horse on an ugly prostitute, and is thus forced to the realization that *eros* turns into *sexus*, adoration into lust. The idealized father surrogate fails miserably—a variation of the motif of the 'crumbling idol' frequent in initiation stories—and the indissoluble contradiction between the experiences of the boy in the two contrastively parallel scenes in the pristine green of the matitudinal race course and in the nocturnal decay of the shabby whorehouse explodes his value system and deprives him of all childlike certainties.

Notes

This article is the slightly revised version of a paper read in December 1978 at the universities of Freiburg, Heidelberg, Stuttgart, and Tübingen.

1. Cf. Hans Heinrich Muchow, *Jugend und Zeitgeist: Morphologie der Kulturpubertät* (Reinbek, 1962), pp. 9–13.

8. "Fable," in *The Hot Gates and Other Occasional Pieces* (London, 1970), p. 88.

9. *The American People: A Study in National Character* (New York, n.d.), p. 121.

10. *Radical Innocence: Studies in the Contemporary American Novel* (New York, 1966), p. 40.

11. Cf. *Teen-Age Tyranny* (New York, 1963).

27. All references are to the text as reprinted in *The Young Man in American Literature: The Initiation Theme*, ed. William Coyle (New York, 1969), pp. 281–288.

> —Peter Freese, "'Rising in the World' and 'Wanting to Know Why': The Socialization Process as Theme of the American Short Story,' *Archiv für das Studium der Neueren Sprachen und Literaturen* 218, no. 2 (1981): pp. 286-88; 294-5.

[Frank Gado is the author of "The Novel in Exile: Types and Patterns" (1982) and editor of *First Person: Conversations on Writers and Writing* (1973). In the following excerpt from the Introduction to his edition of Sherwood Anderson's stories, Gado discusses the narrator's ambivalence and Anderson's departure from the conventional initiation motif.]

If any one coupling of theme and structure in Anderson's short fiction is paradigmatic, it is this progress to a culminative moment in which the reader empathically perceives a character's utter vulnerability and confusion. Anderson employs various strategies toward this end, but behind each lies the universal nightmare of the self discovering its nakedness before the world.

As "I Want to Know Why" shows, this nightmarish quality often arises from a sexual context. The story seems another instance of the initiation motif that is so characteristic of the period's fiction; indeed, one recognizes a number of conventions in its movement from the narrator's expressions of his unwitting wish to remain a child, to a climactic event that simultaneously confirms his innocent intuition and prefigures its inevitable loss, to his bewilderment on discovering his surrogate father's "rottenness." Even so, Anderson departs from the usual pattern: the narrator does not actually become an initiate (none of Anderson's narrators is ever truly initiated into the secrets of the tribe), nor is this adolescent's attainment of sexual sophistication quite the point. Almost by definition, the initiation story proceeds from ignorance to knowledge; here, in contrast, the narrator begins with an account of his sure moral judgment and ends with a confession of his uncertainty. A critical approach to "I Want to Know Why" virtually requires consideration of the reasons for this inversion.

The implications of the conclusion appear self-evident: in kissing the prostitute, Jerry Tillford has shown himself to be just another adult, thereby betraying the narrator's trust in his mentor's moral superiority; furthermore, since Jerry also functions as an older alter-ego, his fall from grace anticipates the narrator's encounter with his own "rottenness" as he advances into manhood. (Thus, it is not only Jerry but also life that betrays the adolescent's innocent faith.) Nothing in the ending violates the reader's expectations; in fact, Anderson has specifically foreshadowed it by having the narrator, early in the story, complain about a trick played on him. An adult had said that eating half a cigar would stunt his growth, but the foul-tasting remedy "did no good. I kept right on growing. It was a joke." The same elements—anger at the treachery of adults, despair over the inability to halt biological change, and fear of not fitting into a mysterious scheme of life—recur in the ending; in effect, it is the joke's complement.

But to see *merely* how this specific joke operates within the story is not enough. The more significant observation, bearing directly on Anderson's unorthodox practice, is that the dynamics of the story itself are joke-like. Humor in general deals figuratively with anxiety, and jokes in particular manifest this anxiety not only in their subject matter but also in their structure. The joke trades in subversion, especially in the punch line's upsetting of assumptions; its action proceeds along a double course that simultaneously confirms and violates its own logic. Although the result is scarcely funny, in "I Want to Know Why," the story develops toward a similar state of contradiction. The narrator urgently wants to "know why," yet, just as urgently, he tries to retreat from that knowledge. The reader immediately knows the "why's" that cause the narrator's distress, yet, from a farther remove, the more profound questions raised about human behavior remain unanswered—and unanswerable. On the one hand, the conclusion implies the reassurance that the narrator's confusion will disappear when, inevitably, he attains the reader's level of sophistication; on the other, it induces a longing for return to innocence.

Although critics commonly speak of Anderson's "ambiguity," the term is seldom appropriate. His characters are often frustrated in their efforts to unriddle their circumstances, but the stories themselves neither turn on the possibility of alternative interpretations nor show their author to be equivocal or unsteady in his purpose. What is mislabeled ambiguity might better be described as a method of "*anti*guity."

—Frank Gado, "Introduction." *The Teller's Tales*, Frank Gado, ed..
(Schenectady, New York: Union College Press 1983): pp. 7-9.

JOHN E. PARISH ON THE SILENT FATHER

[John E. Parish is the author of "Milton and the Well-Fed Angel" (1967) and "Robert Parsons and the English Counter-Reformation" (1966). In the following excerpt from this article, "The Silent Father in 'I Want to Know Why,'" Parish discusses the complex relationship between the narrator and his father.]

I Want to Know Why is no part of the literature of revolt against illusions and is not concerned with repudiating sentimentality; it is curiously conventional in the values it upholds. Though they have thrown welcome light on other aspects of the story, the critics have overlooked one of Anderson's principal aims, which is to show hovering behind the sensitive adolescent an understanding father who loves his son deeply, observes him constantly—from a distance—and wisely says to his wife: "Let him alone." Anderson wholeheartedly endorses this quiet lawyer's philosophy of parental duty and expects his readers always to be aware of him and to admire him greatly. The lawyer is a character hardly less important to the story than the boy himself, who is, in fact, slowly growing into a man like his father.

Extremely permissive? Not if the phrase means imprudently indulgent. "Mother jawed and cried but Pop didn't say much." If the father is less anxious than the mother it is not because he is indifferent or ineffectual but because, having unobtrusively guided his son for fifteen years, he knows him well and has confidence in his good sense and basic integrity. The boy's infatuation with horses and racing is understandable to this parent, who must have lived through a similar passion in his own adolescence and knows that his son too will outgrow it. Unlike many parents of a later generation, he does not feel obligated to feign an enthusiasm equal to his son's; if he risks alienating the boy's affection, he accepts the risk as a duty. He is, one must admit, old-fashioned.

To infer from what the boy says about the father of Henry Rieback that he is disappointed with his own is completely to miss the point. When he says "My own father is a lawyer. He's all right," he is expressing—with natural masculine restraint—full approval; and when he adds "but [he] don't make much money and can't buy me things and anyway I'm getting so old now I don't expect it," he means exactly what he says. There may be some bravado in his voice but there is no resentment, and the tone is predominantly proud, sincere, manly. The reader must see that the father withholds gifts like bicycles and gold watches and Boy Scout uniforms (luxuries a generation ago, which many parents allowed their sons to wait for), not because he cannot provide them, but because he does not need to purchase his son's respect, as does Rieback, and because he is quietly training his son in self-reliance and other values sometimes dismissed as bourgeois. The narrator's statement that his father does not make much money has evidently been taken by the critics to mean that the lawyer is a failure in his profession, but the mature reader ought to hear in this comment echoes from his own childhood, when a father or mother trying to teach him how properly to value material possessions gave such a reason for not indulging a whim. What the father means, if the boy is quoting him, and what the boy in part understands, is that to gratify immediately a yearning for a bicycle or a gold watch or a Scout suit before the boy has learned its worth or worthlessness would be of doubtful wisdom.

This interpretation of the narrator's comparison of his father and the gambler is supported by the fact that when the four boys start out for Saratoga the narrator has thirty-seven dollars and Henry Rieback has eleven. The narrator has earned his money working nights and Saturdays in Enoch Meyer's grocery and has saved it; but the reader is shedding easy tears if he pities him as a child-laborer or indicts his father as improvident. The boy, who feels pride in his accomplishment rather than self-pity, mentally endorses his father's standard of values though, being a boy, naturally he cannot entirely keep from envying Henry the gifts which he has received in lieu of honest parental attention.

The narrator, of course, understands less than the reader should why his father "never said nothing against Henry" or

Henry's father while the fathers of some of his friends were outspoken in their condemnation: "They said to their boys that money so come by is no good and they didn't want their boys brought up to hear gamblers' talk and be thinking about such things and maybe embrace them." The lawyer-father does not want to impose his own opinions on his son. He intends to let the boy form his own moral judgments, though in his own silent example he provides him with a reliable yardstick for measuring other men.

There is proof that the boy has already begun to follow his father's example in this confident declaration: "If I wanted to be a gambler like Henry Rieback's father I could get rich. I know I could and Henry says so too.... That's what I would do if I wanted to be a gambler, but I don't." Here one sees irony in the use of verb *know*. What the boy claims to know for a fact—that he can predict by intuition the outcome of a horse race—is to the reader an obvious untruth. What he claims not to know—in the title sentence and at other points in his story—is a knowledge which he is acquiring unconsciously over the years from the example of his quiet mentor but which he is so far only half willing to face: the knowledge that the men, black and white, who have elected to spend their lives around race tracks are fundamentally irresponsible and inferior to men like his father. The father's wisdom in not forbidding his son to associate with Henry is evident here: the boy still feels the lure of the race tracks and still believes naively that he is endowed with a gift that could make him rich, but he has not been seduced by these attractions.

The disillusionment which the narrator experiences at the farmhouse is not the beginning of his moral development, as Ringe seems to believe; it represents another hurdle of the sort that he has been clearing, one by one, over a number of years— a higher hurdle, certainly, but not an insuperable one. Anderson has made this incident the climax of the story and consequently it looms large, but he has prepared his reader for it by showing how both characters, father and son, have behaved on earlier occasions—occasions which, though briefly treated, should be recognized as episodes in the skillfully constructed plot.

—John E. Parish, "The Silent Father in Anderson's 'I Want To Know Why.'" *Rice University Studies*, (1965): pp. 50-52.

WALTER B. RIDEOUT ON BIOGRAPHY AND FICTION

[Walter B. Rideout is the author of *The Radical Novel in the United States, 1900-1954: Some Interrelations of Literature and Society* (1992) and "Talbot Whittingham and Anderson: A Passage to Winesburg, Ohio" (1976). In the following excerpt from this article, "'I Want to Know Why' As Biography and Fiction," Rideout discusses the blending of biography with fiction.]

"I Want to Know Why" has been read in many ways—as a variation on the Genesis myth of the fall from innocence to experience, as a representation of the ambiguity of good and evil in the world, as a psychological study of a young male's concern over sexuality—but in the context of Anderson's emotional situation at the time he was writing the story in mid-August of 1919 an immediate, personal reading also emerges. Part of what he was transmuting into this fiction was his direct experience of the race track milieu, and bits of that assimilated reality stand out. Very possibly he had seen the thoroughbreds race at Saratoga in the August of 1916 or of 1917 when he was not far away at Chateaugay Lake; but certainly he had learned all he needed to know about "Beckersville" from his occasional visits to Harrodsburg, Kentucky, where two other of his clients, David and Hanley Bohon, sons of a local banker, had become rich in the mail order business through schemes Anderson had suggested to them. Both Beckersville and Harrodsburg are near Lexington in the Blue Grass region, and in both there is, or was, a "Banker Bohon." For the lyrical descriptions of the morning sights, smells, and sounds of the training track Anderson had only to recall nostalgically his boyhood mornings at the track at the Clyde fairgrounds. The names and characteristics of the thoroughbreds required little invention. "Sun Briar" was readily converted into "Sunstreak," of course; and he could draw on his recent memory of watching Sir Barton's five-length win over Billy Kelly at the 1919 Derby for his conception of a horse that before a race was outwardly composed but was "a raging torrent inside." Yet he may have drawn as well on reports concerning a new two-year-old, Man o' War, who was driving the Saratoga fans wild that August with his speed, stamina, and utter will to win; for just as Sunstreak is owned by "Mr. Van Riddle of New York" who has "the biggest farm we've got in our country," so Man o' War was owned by Mr. Sam (Samuel D.) Riddle, a wealthy Pennsylvanian textile manufacturer who had both the Glen Riddle Farm near Philadelphia and the huge Faraway Farm near Lexington. As for the awkward-looking but powerful gelding "Middlestride," Anderson had seen him win at Churchill Downs in 1918 under his real name Exterminator, a gelding well-known for his many victories and his gaunt, unprepossessing appearance, which gave him the affectionate nickname of "Old Bones." (Incidentally, Anderson may have adapted the name Middlestride from Midway, a thoroughbred who, the newspapers reported, had won the Kentucky Handicap at Churchill Downs back in late May, 1919.)

Horses and Negroes would have been much on Anderson's mind in August of 1919, that month not only of the Saratoga thoroughbred meets but also of the Grand Circuit harness races that were moving from Ohio to the East and back to Ohio, carrying with them an intense rivalry among three great drivers—Walter Cox, Tom Murphy, and Anderson's long-time favorite, Pop Geers, the Silent Man from Tennessee, who unlike Jerry Tillford never boasted that it was he, not his trotter or pacer, who won a race. The horses themselves one could depend on; they were embodiments of beautiful motion, courage, a clean honest devotion to the challenge of the race. One could depend too on some, if not all, of the men who worked with the thoroughbreds and hence took on their best qualities. Especially one could depend on the track "niggers" like Bildad Johnson, who intuitively understood horses and horse-crazy boys, and of whom one could say, comparing them with whites: "You can trust them. They are squarer with kids." When "I Want to Know Why" was published in H. L. Mencken's *The Smart Set* in November, 1919, after the terrible summer of race riots in several American cities, it was as though Anderson were declaring publicly which side he had been on.

The praise of blacks might also have been prompted by some memory of Burt, the black groom Sherwood had known in Clyde; but the chances are good that Bildad was in part suggested by Jim in *Huck Finn*, for *Huck* would have been on Anderson's mind that August also. Off and on for over a year he had been talking and corresponding about Twain and his masterpiece with Van Wyck Brooks, who was at the moment writing about that Westerner's ordeal in the East. A Huck Finn cast to the Boy's speech—why else his use of the odd word "fantods"?—would be fitting, given a Bildad Johnson who, though allowed only to cook at the tracks for the white men, is as admirable a figure as Huck's black friend, and given too the picaresque atmosphere of the race track world, which is as much a refuge from conventional society as was the raft on the Mississippi River. As much and no more, for just as life on the raft was vulnerable to invasion by all sorts of human ugliness, so is life at the track. Only a few weeks earlier in Ephraim, Anderson had temporarily planned a group of children's tales, not the usual "asinine sentimental nonsense," as Anderson put it and Twain Might have, but pictures of actual "country life at the edge of a middle-western town"; and "I Want to Know Why," concerned with a boy only a little beyond childhood, was not conceived as sentimental nonsense either. Like Huck Finn of St. Petersburg, Missouri, the fifteen-year-old Boy from Beckersville, Kentucky, is no innocent. He knows a good deal about adult nastiness already—a horse can be "pulled" in a race by a crooked jockey, one can hear "rotten talk" around a livery stable, a "bad woman house" can be found near any race track—but he can submerge such knowledge in his sheer joy at the thoroughbreds and the aura of dedication, beauty, and sensuous delight they cast around themselves. He can submerge it up to the point, that is, that the world of corruption breaks massively in on him.

—Walter B. Rideout, "'I Want to Know Why' As Biography and Fiction," *Midwestern Miscellany* 12, (1984): pp. 10-12.

PLOT SUMMARY OF

"The Egg"

First published in March 1920 in the *Dial*, a non-political monthly journal of arts and letters, "The Egg" which takes its name from the volume's title, *The Triumph of the Egg*, is a very complex and humorous Sherwood Anderson story. As Anderson's Memoirs and autobiographies document, he was both very fond and equally vulnerable to the vicissitudes of little magazines. Indeed, this story established Anderson's gift for humor or, as some critics have said, his ability to understand the tragi-comic. Proof of Anderson's critical acclaim from the international literary world is evidenced in Virignia Woolf's 1925 essay on American fiction: "In the *Triumph of the Egg* there is some rearrangement of the old elements of art which makes us rub our eyes. ... Mr. Anderson has bored into that deeper and warmer layer of human nature which it would be frivolous to ticket new or old, American or European." "The Egg" has also been widely anthologized and dramatized in both a one-act play by Raymond O'Neil for the Provincetown Players and presented as a curtain raiser for Eugene O'Neill's *Diff'rent* in New York on February 10, 1925. The story explores the frustrations of one of Anderson's displaced persons, a grotesque for whom life is a sequence of failures and frustrations as he attempts to become a success as defined by the values of society.

Again, as in "I Want to Know Why," Anderson uses an adolescent narrator, the son of a grotesque, who tells us that his father is a farm hand working for one Thomas Butterworth near the town of Bidwell, Ohio. The narrator also states that he assumes his father was "intended by nature to be a cheerful, kindly man," an assumption which also leaves open the possibility at the conclusion of the story his father will prove to be just the opposite. Essentially a loner, "quite happy with his position in life," the narrator states that "[h]e had at that time no notion of trying to rise in the world." But something happens to disrupt his father's complacency, a transformation which results from marrying in his thirty-fifth year and, by extension, leading a more conventional lifestyle. The newlyweds suddenly become ambitious when "[t]he American passion for getting up in the world took possession of them." After all, this change in perspective may be attributable to his mother, a schoolteacher, whom we may presume to be better educated, and who has access to the constant influx of political and social trends. Nevertheless, even his mother cannot be entirely to blame as "she wanted nothing. For father and myself she was incurably ambitious." It is important to recognize that, from the outset, although the narrator is sympathetic, he is also very uncertain about what to make of the story he is about to relate and that, in the end, he will only be able to speculate on the cause of his father's failures and ultimate despair. Indeed, the narrator's inability to place responsibility is yet another manifestation of the interpersonal distance and utter isolation from which each of the characters appears to be suffering. It is not by accident that the narrator is even distanced from his parents, referring to them as "the two people."

The couple's first venture disappoints as the inhospitable land they purchase dooms them to failure in the chicken farming business. This business failure forms a lasting and unforgettable experience upon the adolescent narrator. "I grew into boyhood on the place and got my first impressions of life there. From the beginning they were impressions of disaster and if, in my turn, I am a gloomy man inclined to see the darker side of life, I attribute it to the fact that ... the happy joyous days of childhood were spent on a chicken farm." Yet, the tragic circumstances of a childhood are balanced by the "tragic" facts surrounding the life of a chicken. "It is born out of an egg, lives for a few weeks as a tiny fluffy thing such as you will see pictured on Easter cards, then becomes hideously naked ... gets diseases ... [and then] stands looking with stupid eyes at the sun, becomes sick and dies." Indeed, the description of the chickens conforms to Anderson's all-pervasive notion of the grotesque and they do indeed seem to be extensions of their human caretakers. "Grotesques are borne out of eggs as out of people." But, lest we lose sight of the genuine bathos of the story, the narrator cannot help but give us a hilarious commentary on various documented accounts which extol the virtues of chicken farming. "It is intended to be read by the gods who have just eaten of tree of the knowledge of good and evil.... Do not be led astray by it. It was not written for you."

When the narrator finally returns to his story, he tells us that his focus will be on the subject of the egg. After the years of futile effort on the chicken farm, the family moves into the town of Bidwell, Ohio to partake in the restaurant business. But the picture planted in our minds by the young narrator is that this next venture will likewise be doomed to failure. Despite the comic rendition of their migration into town in a borrowed wagon, replete with "legs of cheap chairs and at the back of the pile of beds, tables, and boxes filled with kitchen utensils ... a crate of live chickens, and on top of that a baby carriage," there is the strong suggestion that an already determined failure looms over the desperate attempt of this family to break free. Furthermore, it is also suggested that the fate of these besieged chickens is hopelessly and inextricably caught up in the destiny of their human owners. They are, indeed, one big and impoverished family, the narrator informing us that the ten desolate years at the chicken farm were spent in pursuit of ineffective remedies to cure chicken diseases with such "medications" as "Wilmer's White Wonder Cholera Cure" and "Professor Bidlow's Egg Producer." And from the advertisement of these ridiculous cures which were to be found in "poultry papers," the narrator launches into an equally fanciful description of his father's bald head, which digression, for all its humor, underscores the core tragedy of the story that it is destined to remain an unattainable and unrealizable desire. "I fancied, something like a broad road, such a road as Caesar might have made on which to lead his legions out of Rome and into the wonders of an unknown world.... a far beautiful place where there were no chicken farms and where life was a happy eggless affair." But perhaps the most extreme, albeit comical, expression of a fruitless longing is contained in the fact that his father insists on embalming deformed chickens in alcohol. "He had some sort of notion that if he could but bring into henhood or roosterhood a five-legged hen or two-headed rooster his fortune would be made."

When the family reaches its final destination, it is a town at the foot of a hill, a mile away from the railway station in a place called Pickleville—a name which is an apt description of the deformed chickens his father preserves in bottles of alcohol. As it turns out, there was a former cider mill and pickle factory in a distant past. And so the family settles in Pickleville, ostensibly to enter the restaurant business. Nevertheless, there is a second and more important agenda as it is his mother's desire that her son attend one of the better schools to be found in town and thereby make a place for himself in the world. But this vision of a better life for her son seems likewise inevitably doomed to desire based on the narrator's description of unworthiness to be happy. "I was afraid of being seen in my gay mood. It must have seemed to me that I was doing a thing which should not be done by one who, like myself, had been raised on a chicken farm where death was a daily visitor."

And while the father grows ambitious, this fate of daily visitations with death is now imposed on the customers in the family's newly-opened diner. His father insists on displaying his collection of preserved deformed chickens to the customers, eager to take "the bottles containing the poultry monstrosities down from their place on the shelf," to the point of making one of the customers sick "by the sight of the terribly deformed bird floating in the alcohol." This customer is the young Joe Kane, whom the narrator's father is determined to provide with "public entertainment" in addition to coffee and sandwiches. When the sight of this "freak show" has the opposite effect and alienates Joe, the father, unable to understand where he went wrong, continues to exacerbate the situation with the promise of performing an impossible sleight-of-hand by forcing an egg into a bottle without breaking the shell. "He worked and worked and a spirit of desperate determination took possession of him.... Father made a last desperate effort to conquer the egg and make it do the thing that would establish his reputation as one who knew how to entertain guests who came into the restaurant." But, alas, the experiment in social interaction ends in abject failure. Anderson has probed beneath the surface of the ridiculous to show the man to be as hideous as his deformed chickens, a deformity which will only end in death. And, more importantly, we come to understand that the young and unsuspecting narrator will inherit the same inescapable fate that his father has been condemned to live out. "I wondered why eggs had to be and why from the egg came the hen who laid the egg. ... At any rate, the problem remains unsolved in my mind." Isolation and frustration simply cannot be transcended because no one in this family understands why they are trapped within or how they may escape from the self-perpetuating cycle of a hopeless inability to communicate.

LIST OF CHARACTERS IN

"The Egg"

The **Adolescent narrator** relates the humorous story of growing up on a farm and later moving to Pickleville. Happy to have left the farm, he goes to school in town, thereby managing to avoid his family's far-fetched plans. He is also able to provide a more detached and observant commentary on the ridiculous schemes his father gets involved in.

The **Narrator's father** is a farmer who later enters the restaurant business, a failure at both vocations. A good example of Anderson's notion of the grotesque, he is the victim of his own self-deception in believing that he can transform his coffee shop into a festive establishment by entertaining his customers with his own brand of magic.

Joe Kane is a young customer whom the father fails to entertain and engage.

CRITICAL VIEWS ON
"The Egg"

MICHAEL D. WEST ON ANDERSON'S TRIUMPH

[Michael D. West is the author of "Transcendental Wordplay: America's Romantic Punsters and the Search for the Language of Nature" (2000). In the following excerpt from his earlier article, "Sherwood Anderson's Triumph: 'The Egg,'" West discusses those aspects of the story which illustrate Anderson's triumph as a writer.]

This essay is undertaken in the conviction that within the confines of a half-dozen or so stories, and there only, Anderson is a truly memorable writer. The inferior quality of the rest of Anderson's writing and the overshadowing popularity of "I'm a Fool," the anthologists' delight, have combined to obscure the merits of his best stories. In particular, Anderson's masterpiece "The Egg," the subject of this study, has never received the sort of attention it deserves. Its complexity repays close analysis as richly as the best of *Dubliners*. (...)

Early reviewers often singled out the story for praise and all modern interpretive biographies recognize its surpassing merit. James Schevill terms it "one of Anderson's greatest stories and one of the outstanding tales in American literature," and Irving Howe states flatly that "of all Anderson's short fictions 'The Egg' most deserves to be placed among the great stories of the world."[20] Yet, hampered by space, critics of the story have dealt only haphazardly with the reasons for its greatness. Even Howe's admirable discussion relies heavily on plot synopsis and cites but one detail to demonstrate that the story is "complex and ironic." Assuming familiarity with the plot as a point of departure, I hope to substantiate the more acute perceptions embodied in the scanty critical literature on the story.

Anderson's greatest fault as a prose stylist is his saturation in the facile, vaguely evocative phrases of advertising. It saps his command of colloquial expression. But in "The Egg" this facility becomes a virtue. Only an adman could have created the pathetic touch of the father's naively simple, straightforward and honest sign, EAT HERE, "the command that was so seldom obeyed." Anderson knew that it takes a come-on to bring in the customers; on top of his paint factory in Elyria was the sign, ROOF-FIX: SEND FOR FREE CATALOG. Or take the words with which the father introduces his attempt to bottle the egg: "People will want to know how you got the egg in the bottle. Don't tell them. Keep them guessing. That is the way to have fun with this trick." The short, choppy sentences and the awkward and unidiomatic failure to contract *that is* perfectly mimic the prose of the cheap pamphlets promising, to teach you One Hundred and One Easy Tricks which is also the prose of the cheap mail-order catalogues that vend them. Flow moving the tyro entertainer's parrot-like repetition of his patter! A curious coincidence enables us to see exactly how in this story Anderson's mail-order prose (his specialty as a copywriter) is transmuted. Alyse Gregory quite properly stigmatized the effusively meaningless language in which Anderson's ideals are often couched, such as the vague phrase "a kind of white wonder of life."[21] Pure Anderson, admittedly, and pure tin—but note how the same combination of words appears in "The Egg": "Wilmer's White Wonder Cholera Cure ... advertised in the poultry papers." Clearly, Anderson's often shoddy lyricism derives from his advertising background; but, just as clearly, in this story the lyric impulse is mastered and directed ironically against that background. Consider in this light the paired adjectives in each of the following sentences:

> If, in my turn, I am a gloomy man inclined to see the darker side of life, I attribute it to the fact that what should have been for me the happy joyous days of childhood were spent on a chicken farm.
>
> I ... dreamed I was a tiny thing going along the road into a far beautiful place where there were no chicken farms.
>
> It is a hopeful literature and declares that much may be done by simple ambitious people who own a few hens.
>
> In the evening bright happy groups would come singing down Turner's Pike.

In *Mid-American Chants* Anderson tries to make serious statements in language of such falsified simplicity. Here, the phrases are used, without exception, ironically.

Another strand woven into the irony of "The Egg" is the frequent Biblical phraseology. Anderson publicized his indebtedness to the Bible by tearing pages out of the copies placed in hotel rooms. But when he attempts to use it as a conscious framework, it constricts rather than inspires his imagination, as in the story of Jesse Bentley, the most unsatisfactory section of *Winesburg*. In "The Egg," however, Scriptural echoes, beautifully diffused, expand the significance of the characters and their actions. At times the language is not strictly Biblical but merely has an archaic flavor: "in the days of her lying in." Sometimes the echo is more specific; the chicken "born out of an egg" that "lives for a few weeks as a tiny fluffy thing ... stands looking with stupid eyes at the sun, becomes sick and dies" does so to the cadences of Job's *Man that is born of woman*. "One might write a book concerning our flight from the chicken-farm into town" suggests, as well as the flight of an army and that of chickens, the Flight into Egypt. Significantly, the first chapters of Genesis bulk largest in Anderson's consciousness. Literature on chicken farms should "be read by the gods who have just eaten of the tree of the knowledge of good and evil." Repeated references to the sweat on the father's brow enhance the meaning of his small life: *In the sweat of thy face shalt thou eat bread*. And the crucial incident of the story is given a weird resonance by the slaying of Abel. After the father has offered the *firstlings of his flock*, Kane's amused rejection of him, though understandable, is also a re-enactment of Cain's murder. This is, of course, in no sense the "meaning" of the scene; the great effectiveness of the Scriptural echoes in this story lies in the fact that they occur with evocative rather than informative value, and with a touch of irony. The father is, after all, the personification of the un-Abel, and there is a twist in having the man whom we know as the "innkeeper" and "restaurant keeper" aspiring to be his *brother's keeper*.

NOTES

20. Schevill, p. 164; Howe, p. 168.

21. *The Triumph of the Egg* (New York, 1921), p. 237. The phrase occurs in his most characteristically and revealingly bad story, "Out of Nowhere into Nothing." It describes the

experience that overtakes the heroine of the story, Rosalind Westcott, spreadeagled on the ground in an orchard while she feels "something that had nothing to do with the ground beneath her or the trees or the clouds in the sky, that seemed to want to come to her, come into her," to wit, "white wonder." Actually, Alyse Gregory cites another use of the phrase, the context of which I have not been able to locate: "filled with the white wonder of it." Anderson's use of the phrase is, as its occurrence in "The Egg" shows, a capsule history of the fate of Emersonian Transcendentalism.

—Michael D. West, "Sherwood Anderson's Triumph: 'The Egg,'" *American Quarterly* 20, no. 4, (Winter 1968): pp. 676; 680-82.

N. Bryllion Fagin on the Thematic Structure

[N. Bryllion Fagin is the author of *Poe as a Literary Critic* (1946) and *William Bartram: Interpreter of the American Landscape* (1935). In the following excerpt from his book, *The Phenomenon of Sherwood Anderson*, Fagin discusses mechanical lives of the characters.]

Winesburg, Ohio, is a thoughtful book. "There is a time in the life of every boy when he for the first time takes the backward view of life. Perhaps that is the moment when he crosses the line into manhood." *Winesburg* signifies the arrival of this time in the life of America. It is a backward view of life; it is the crossing of the line into manhood. And just as to the boy George Willard "the sadness of sophistication" had come, just so do we find the sadness of sophistication in the work of Anderson. *Winesburg* is a sad book; a book of drab little stories, a book of the tragedy of our life. And yet it is a happy book. Its appearance was a happy omen. It is a tribute to the sturdiness of the spirit of a people. It is a landmark in the evolution of a mature literature. "One shudders," remarks Anderson, "at the thought of the meaninglessness of life while at the same instant, and if the people of the town are his people, one loves life so intensely that tears come into the eyes." *Winesburg* is a book of passionate revolt—revolt which is always an expression of a deep love of life.

In *The Triumph of the Egg* (1921), we have a few short stories whose strength cannot be disputed, even by those critics for whom Sherwood Anderson is a personification of evil. The first story, "I Want to Know Why," is undoubtedly one of the finest short stories ever produced by an American artist. In it we have Anderson's almost uncanny understanding of the adolescent boy and Anderson's love of horses. Beauty burns, in its own way, in its own ideal. "There isn't anything as sweet as that horse!" the boy narrator cries out. "He stands at the post quiet and not letting on, but he is just burning up inside ... it makes you ache to see him. It hurts you." The man who can ride this horse, the man who communes with beauty, is truly a god. But gods totter. Gods may have no beauty inside. Jerry Tillford may be the jockey of "Sunstreak" but he has enough earthiness to entertain on his lap a vulgar woman of the streets. Gods totter. And then, "at the tracks the air don't taste as good, or smell as good. It is because a man like Jerry Tillford, who knows what he does, could see a horse like 'Sunstreak' run and kiss a woman like that the same day.... I keep thinking about it and it spoils looking at the horses and smelling things and hearing niggers laugh and everything.... What did he do it for? I want to know why." A first encounter with Reality. A truly great short story.

There are other memorable stories in this book. Stories written with passion, with fire that almost scorches. Stories that reach out, searching, corroding, into the tissues of our life. There is "The Other Woman" and "The Egg"; "Unlighted Lamps"; "Brothers"; and finally "Out of Nowhere Into Nothing." There are, of course, a few inconsequential stories—mere artistic exercises and unsuccessful allegories.

In a way, "Out of Nowhere Into Nothing" summarizes all phases of Sherwood Anderson's work. In this story we have a recapitulation of his manner and his substance. Here we have the inarticulateness of character that we found in *Winesburg*. Here we have again the dreariness of *Main Street*. "Willow Spring was a rather meaningless, dreary town, one of thousands of such towns in Indiana, Illinois, Wisconsin, Kansas, Iowa...." Here we have the Andersonian conviction that "I have always missed life. It always goes away from me." Here we have the rebellion against our commercial success, in which there is "a deep-seated vulgarity involved...." Here we have the thought of the battle of the sexes. "Was it the fate of women to be consumed by men, and of men to be consumed by women?" (Reminiscent of Strindberg. Our literature is catching up. Our life is evoking old motifs.) Here we have the consciousness that "perhaps I am learning to think." ("Tinking is hard," complains O'Neill's *Hairy Ape*. It is, when one—man or nation—is learning.) And finally we have Anderson himself in the figure of Melville Stoner, who "would not write as others do" and who has come to a conviction that "we know little enough here in America, either in the towns or in the cities ... we are all on the rush. We are all for action. I sit still and think.... I'd tell what every one thought. It would startle people, frighten them a little, eh?"

Anderson has succeeded. He has startled people. He does not write as others have done. He is "an artist working with a repulsive medium. Repulsive to whom? To the public at large."[1] *The Triumph of the Egg* discloses once more all of Anderson's peculiar gifts, his remarkable kinship with the life of his nation and his time. Only a blind public can say that he works in a repulsive medium, a public blinded by "old thoughts and beliefs planted by dead men" ("Seeds"). Anderson's stories are a call—a prophetic call—to life and beauty, to the nobility of life.

> "I said they might build temples to their lives.
> I threw my words at faces floating in a street.
>
> I said that life was life, that men in streets and
>   cities might build temples to their souls.
> I said they might build temples to themselves."

Horses and Men (1923) contains nine "tales, long and short, from our American life." They are a continuation of Anderson's quest. One feels the wonder of the phenomenon of these stories. A man still searching, after seven crowded years of creative effort, "with these nervous and uncertain hands ... for the form of things concealed in the darkness." Sometimes he finds it; sometimes he does not. But even the failures are arresting, sharp, passionate.

NOTE

1. Joseph Collins, *Taking the Literary Pulse*. George H. Doran Co.

—N. Bryllion Fagin, "The Liberator of Our Short Story." *The Phenomenon of Sherwood Anderson* (Baltimore: The Rosi-Bryn Company, 1927; New York: Russell & Russell, reissued 1973): pp. 86-90.

DAVID R. MESHER ON THE TRIUMPH OF ANDERSON'S EGO

[David R. Mesher is the author of "Science and Technology in Modern British Fiction: The Two Cultures" (1984) and "Kay Boyle: An Eightieth Birthday Interview" (1983). In the following excerpt from his article, "A Triumph of the Ego in Anderson's 'The Egg,'" Mesher discusses the redemptive aspects of this story in Sherwood Anderson's personal history.]

Sherwood Anderson's two best stories, "Death in the Woods" and "The Egg," share an odd but central detail: the narrator's open admission that he has fabricated the most important elements of the story he is telling.

Nevertheless, in "Death in the Woods," the narrator does attempt a realistic explanation of his knowledge. He has seen the woman's body in the snow, he says, and had heard "the whispered comments of the men" at the scene, and "lator, in town ... must have heard other fragments of the old woman's story. The narrator of "The Egg" is much more straightforward about the story of his father and Joe Kane. "for some unexplainable reason," he claims, "I know the story as well as though I had been a witness to my father's discomfiture." Yet as astute a reader as Irving Howe, who faults "Death in the Woods; for a lesser imposition on his willing suspension of disbelief, ignores this inexplicability and says only that "the narrator, deliberately avoiding a direct dramatic line, then tells what happened in the store below." "The Egg has usually been read, by Howe and others, as an autobiographical expression of Anderson's relationship with his father and, on a larger scale, "as a parable of human defeat"—meaning, of course, the defeat of the narrator's father. But, if the parallel with "Death in the Woods holds, "The Egg is a story about not the father but the son who, as narrator-turned-creator, projects the reality of his own psychology onto the history of his subject.

In "Death in the Woods," Anderson prepares his reader for the coming departure from narrative conventions at the beginning of the story. Though the details of the woman's background are not such as would require a great deal of personal knowledge, the narrator makes a point of recalling them, or in Lawry's term "recovering" them, with the justification that "all country and small town people have seen such old women": at the same time, however, the narrator also undercuts the most common details of his tale by continuing, "but no one knows much about them." A different technique is employed in "The Egg" to achieve the same undercutting effect. The story begins with a romanticized portrait of the father's bachelorhood as a farm hand. At this early point, assertions like "he had then a horse of his won and on Saturday evenings drove into town to spend a few hours in social intercourse with other farm hands" seems unremarkable. But as the narrator turns from rather to mother, he passes from assertion to assumption, even though the specifics to be assumed about the mother are far more probably than the details presented as facts about the father. "At ten o'clock," wer are told indicatively, "father drove home along a lonely country road, made his horse comfortable for the night and himself went to bed, quite happy in his position in life." But n discussing his mother and how, after marriage, "the American passion for getting up in the world took possession" of his parents, the narrator inundates us with subjunctives and conditionals:

> It may have been that mother was responsible. Being a school teacher she had no doubt read books and magazines. She had, I presume, read of how Garfield, Lincoln, and other

Americans rose from poverty to fame and greatness and as I lay beside her—in the days of her lying-in—she may have dreamed that I would some day rule men and cities.

The narrator's definite knowledge of the precise and orderly actions of a drunken farm hand, as opposed to his assumption that a school teacher has read books and magazines, has two effects. First, it immediately identifies the sons with his father; second, it distances him from his mother, who has introduced ambition into her husband's previously idyllic existence.

And yet, one might argue, the story centers on neither mother nor son, but on the father, who carries the malformed chickens, "preserved in alcohol and put each in its own glass bottle," from the chicken ranch to the restaurant, the family's next venture. "The grotesques were, he declared, valuable. People, he said, like to look at strange and wonderful things." Human grotesques are similarly valuable to Anderson, who uses them to depict alienation from modern society. But the father's attempts to exhibit his grotesques, especially later for Joe Kane, are futile. Instead, we have the narrator exhibiting his father as a grotesque, a human failure shaped by naïve belief in the American dream – and Anderson depicting his own grotesque, the narrator himself. Thus, even when the narrator is discussing his father, the story is still focused on the son.

The key to the narrator's personality is given in the last line of the story, where he describes "the complete and final triumph of the egg—at least as far as my family is concerned." He says "family" to include himself, even though the events of the story occur while he is a boy; in no direct way do we have a defeat of the narrator. The line only makes literal sense when we understand the events as reconstructions of a defeated mind seeking to place the seeds of his defeat—and the blame for it—as far from himself as possible. If the problem originates with his parents, then the solution would be an imaginative negation of their marriage—a wish that finds expression in the idealized bachelorhood of his father as described in the beginning of the story.

On another level, however, where the egg is the narrator's symbol, the triumph at the end is his as well. And the "defeat"— not "of" but only "concerning" his family—is ambiguous enough to allow for this. Not his parents but the system is the ultimate villain for the narrator, and his triumph against it consists simply of recognizing its dangers and refusing to become involved in it. Willed abstention may take a form no more consequential than an interruption in the cycle of the chicken and the egg; but in it, the narrator finds exoneration of his father than himself.... In "The Egg," the negative attributes of self are characterized by the ambition the narrator forgoes; and through the telling of his largely invented story, the narrator has come not only to knowledge and acceptance of himself, but of others as well.

—David R. Mesher, "A Triumph of the Ego in Anderson's 'The Egg.'" *Studies in Short Fiction*, vol. 17 (1980): pp. 180-83.

Sherwood Anderson

Windy McPherson's Son, 1916
Marching Men, 1917
Mid-American Chants, 1918
Winesburg, Ohio, 1919
Poor White, 1920
The Triumph of the Egg, 1921
Horses and Men, 1923
Many Marriages, 1923
A Story Teller's Story, 1924
Dark Laughter, 1925
The Modern Writer, 1925
Sherwood Anderson's Notebook, 1926
Tar: A Midwest Childhood, 1926
A New Testament, 1927
Alice and the Lost Novel, 1929
Hello Towns!, 1929
Nearer the Grass Roots, 1929
The American County Fair, 1930
Perhaps Women, 1931
Beyond Desire, 1932
Death in the Woods, 1933
No Swank, 1934
Puzzled America, 1935
Kit Brandon, 1936
Plays, Winesburg and Others, 1937
Home Town, 1940
Sherwood Anderson's Memoirs, 1942
The Sherwood Anderson Reader, 1947
Letters of Sherwood Anderson, 1953
Sherwood Anderson's Short Stories, 1962
*Return to Winesburg: Selections from Four Years of Writing
       for a Country Newspaper*, 1967
The Buck Fever Papers, 1971
Correspondence Sherwood Anderson/Gertrude Stein, 1972
The Writer's Book 2, 1975
Sherwood Anderson's Early Writings, 1989
Anderson's Secret Love Letters, 1991
Certain Things Last: Selected short stories of Sherwood Anderson, 1992

WORKS ABOUT
Sherwood Anderson

Abcarian, Richard. "Innocence and Experience in *Winesburg, Ohio.*" *University Review* 35 (Winter 1968): 95-105.

Anderson, David E., ed. *Sherwood Anderson: Dimensions of His Literary Art: A Collection of Critical Essays.* East Lansing: Michigan State University Press, 1976.

———, ed. *Critical Essays on Sherwood Anderson.* Boston: G.K. Hall, 1981.

———. *Sherwood Anderson: An Introduction and Interpretation.* New York: Holt, Rinehart & Winston, 1967.

Appel, Paul P., ed. *Homage to Sherwood Anderson: 1876-1941.* Mamaroneck, N.Y.: Paul P. Appel, 1970.

Bredahl, A. Carl. "'The Young Within': Divided Narrative and Sherwood Anderson's *Winesburg, Ohio.*" *Midwest Quarterly* 27 (1986): 422-37.

Burbank, Rex. *Sherwood Anderson.* New Haven: College & University Press, 1964.

Campbell, Hilbert H., and Charles E. Modlin, eds. *Sherwood Anderson: Centennial Studies.* Troy, N.Y.: Whitson, 1976.

Ciancio, Ralph. "'The Sweetness of the Twisted Apples': Unity of Vision in *Winesburg, Ohio.*" *PMLA* 87 (1972): 994-1006.

Crowley, John W., ed. *New Essays on "Winesburg, Ohio."* Cambridge: Cambridge University Press, 1990.

Dahlberg, Edward. *Alms for Oblivion: Essays by Edward Dahlberg.* Minneapolis: University of Minnesota Press: 3-19.

Ennis, Stephen C. "The Implied Community of *Winesburg, Ohio.*" *The Old Northwest* 11 (1985): 51-60.

Fetterly, Judith, ed. "Growing Up Male in America: 'I Want to Know Why.'" *The Resisting Reader: A Feminist Approach to American Fiction,* 12-22. Bloomington: Indiana University Press, 1978.

Flanagan, John T. "Hemingway's Debt to Sherwood Anderson." *Journal of English and Germanic Philology* 54 (October, 1955): 507-20.

Fussell, Edwin. "*Winesburg, Ohio*: Art and Isolation." *Modern Fiction Studies* 6 (Summer 1960): 106-14.

Gado, Frank, ed. *Sherwood Anderson: The Teller's Tales.* Schenectady, N.Y.: Union College Press, 1983.

Geismar, Maxwell. *The Last of the Provincials: The American Novel.* Boston: Houghton Mifflin, 1947: 223-84.

Hansen, Harry. *Midwest Portraits: A Book of Memories and Friendships.* New York: Harcourt, Brace, 1923: 109-79.

Hoffman, Frederick J. *Freudianism and the Literary Mind.* Baton Rouge: Louisiana State University, 1957: 229-50.

Ingram, Forest L., ed. *Representative Short Story Cycles of the Twentieth Century: Studies in a Literary Genre.* The Hague: Mouton, 1971.

Love, Glen A. "*Winesburg, Ohio* and the Rhetoric of Silence." *American Literature* 40 (March 1968): 38-57.

Luedtke, Luther S. "Sherwood Anderson, Thomas Hardy, and 'Tandy.'" *Modern Fiction Studies* 20 (Winter 1974-1975): 531-40.

Miller, William V. "Earth-Mothers, Succubi, and Other Ectoplasmic Spirits: The Women in Sherwood Anderson's Short Stories." *Midamerica* 1 (1973): 64-81.

Papinchak, Robert Allen. *Sherwood Anderson: A Study of the Short Fiction.* New York: Twayne Publishers, 1992.

———. "'Something in the Elders': The Recurrent Imagery in *Winesburg, Ohio.*" *Winesburg Eagle* 9, no. 1 (November 1983): 1-7.

Phillips, William L. "How Sherwood Anderson Wrote *Winesburg, Ohio.*" *American Literature* 23 (1951): 7-30.

Rideout, Walter B. "The Simplicity of Winesburg, Ohio." *Shenandoah* 13 (Spring 1962): 20-31.

———, ed. *Sherwood Anderson: A Collection of Critical Essays.* Englewood Cliffs, N.J.: Prentice-Hall, 1974.

———. "'The Tale of Perfect Balance': Sherwood Anderson's 'The Untold Lie.'" *Newberry Library Bulletin* 6 (1971): 243-50.

Rosenfeld, Paul. "Sherwood Anderson." *Dial* 72 (1922): 29-42.

San Juan, Epifanio, Jr. "Vision and Reality: A Reconsideration of Sherwood Anderson's *Winesburg, Ohio.*" *American Literature* 35 (May 1963): 137-55.

Schevill, James. *Sherwood Anderson: His Life and Work*. Denver: University of Denver Press, 1951.

Small, Judith Jo. *A Reader's Guide to the Short Stories of Sherwood Anderson*. New York: Hall, 1994.

Spencer, Benjamin T. "Sherwood Anderson: American Mythopoeist." *American Literature* 41 (March 1969): 1-19.

Stouck, David. *"Winesburg, Ohio* and the Failure of Art." *Twentieth Century Literature* 15 (October 1969): 145-51.

———. *"Winesburg, Ohio* as a Dance of Death." *American Literature* 48 (1977): 525-42.

Sutton, William A. *The Road to Winesburg: A Mosaic of the Imaginative Life of Sherwood Anderson*. Metuchen, N.J.: Scarecrow Press, 1972.

Taylor, Welford Dunaway. *Sherwood Anderson*. New York: Ungar, 1977.

Townsend, Kim. *Sherwood Anderson*. Boston: Houghton Mifflin, 1987

Twentieth Century Literature, Sherwood Anderson Issue 23 (February 1977).

Walcutt, Charles Child. *American Literary Naturalism, A Divided Stream*. Minneapolis: University of Minnesota Press, 1964: 222-39.

White, Ray Lewis, ed. *Sherwood Anderson: A Reference Guide*. Boston: G.K. Hall, 1977.

———, ed. *Sherwood Anderson: Essays in Criticism*. Chapel Hill, N.C.: University of North Carolina Press, 1966.

———. "Of Time and *Winesburg, Ohio*: An Experiment in Chronology." *Modern Fiction Studies* 25 (1979-80): 658-66.

———. *"Winesburg, Ohio": An Exploration*. Boston: Twayne, 1990.

Williams, Kenny J. *A Story Teller and a City*. Dekalb: Northern Illinois University Press, 1988.

ACKNOWLEDGMENTS

"Wanderers and Sojourners: Sherwood Anderson and the People of Weinsburg" by David D. Anderson. From *MidAmerica* 22. © 1995 by MidAmerica. Reprinted by permission.

"'I Belong in Little Towns:' Sherwood Anderson's Small Town Post-Modernism" by Clarence Lindsay. From *MidAmerica* XXVI. © 1999 by MidAmerica. Reprinted by permission.

"Sherwood Anderson's Mastery of Narrative Distance" by Paul P. Somers, Jr. From *Twentieth Century Literature* 23, no.1. © 1977 by *Twentieth Century Literature*. Reprinted by permission.

Dewey, Joseph. No God in the Sky and No God in Myself: 'Godliness' and Anderson's *Winesburg*. *Modern Fiction Studies* 35: 2 (1989), 251-253. © Purdue Research Foundation. Reprinted with permission of The Johns Hopkins University Press.

"The Identity of Anderson's Fanatical Farmer," by Robert H. Sykes. From *Studies in Short Fiction*, vol. 18, no. 1. © 1981 by *Studies in Short Fiction*. Reprinted by permission.

"Godliness and the American Dream in Winesburg, Ohio" by Rosemary M. Laughlin. From *Twentieth Century Literature*, vol. 13, no. 2. © 1967 by Hofstra University Press. Reprinted by permission.

"Anderson Writ Large: 'Godliness' in *Winesburg, Ohio*" by John O'Neill. From *Twentieth Century Literature*, vol. 23, no. 1. © 1977 by *Twentieth Century Literature*. Reprinted by permission.

"'Beyond Human Understanding': Confusion and the Call in Winesburg, Ohio" by Thomas Wetzel. From *Midamerica* 23. © 1996 by MidAmerica. Reprinted by permission.

Colquitt, Clare. The Reader as Voyeur: Complicitous Transformation in 'Death in the Woods'. *Modern Fiction Studies* 32:2 (1986), 175-179. Purdue Research Foundation. Reprinted with permission of The Johns Hopkins University Press.

INDEX OF
Themes and Ideas